# The Complete Guide to Rope Techniques

## Nigel Shepherd

D1394655

Constable • London

Constable Publishers
3 The Lanchesters
162 Fulham Palace Road
London W6 9ER
www.constablerobinson.com

This combined edition first published in
the UK by Constable, an imprint of
Constable & Robinson,Ltd 2001

Reprinted 2003

*A Manual of Modern Rope Techniques* first
published by Constable 1990
Copyright © 1990 Nigel Shepherd

*Further Modern Rope Techniques* first
published by Constable 1998
Copyright © 1998 Nigel Shepherd

A copy of the British Library Cataloguing
in Publication Data is available from the
British Library.

ISBN 1-84119-323-2

Printed and bound in the UK

# Notes on Photography

The pictures have been staged to show the set-up for each rope technique in the clearest form possible. To achieve this, clutter has been eliminated by omitting harnesses in many of the pictures. I have replaced the harness in such pictures with a quick draw to depict the tie on point. This is not to be interpreted as a tie on to the abseil loop of the harness unless a karabiner is shown. Where the rope is tied through the quick draw you must assume that this is representative of the harness tie on loops through which you would normally thread the rope when tying on.

A garland twined from varied
waifs and strays

The flowers of thoughtless
youth and later days.

T. C. S. Corry
*Irish Lyrics, Songs and Poems 1879*

# Introduction

This book brings together two earlier volumes, *A Manual of Modern Rope Techniques* and *Further Modern Rope Techniques*, to form the fullest guide to ropework yet published. In these pages you will find a whole host of ideas and suggestions that will hopefully make your climbing a safer experience.

The guide covers everything from basic tying on and belaying methods through to more advanced ropework, and also provides information on simple and more complex self-rescue scenarios on both cliff and glacier. It goes further in offering advice to those who pursue the climbing instructor and SPA awards – qualifications that require a broad base of safe ropework skills to care for others on mountains and crags.

This comprehensive coverage of such a broad subject is dealt with in as simplistic a manner as possible. Each scenario is broken down into its individual components and the solution is drawn from a repertoire of useful techniques that might be applied.

It might be argued that a great deal more could be said about the various techniques and in one sense I would agree. Yet I also believe that to prescribe an unerring solution to a particular problem stifles the imagination, is dogmatic and furthermore takes away that most valuable of learning experiences – self-discovery. If you find a better way to do something I say 'good on yer', and if this book helped you to do that then it has achieved part of its purpose.

Do not encumber yourself with too much extra gadgetry. The techniques in this book are described for normal day-to-day climbing and only require normal day-to-day equipment. 'The more man possesses over and above that which he needs, the more careworn he becomes.' Keep life simple and light.

Most of the techniques described will need lots of practice before you can truly say you know how to implement them. Don't wait for something to go wrong and then expect to be able to recall the page number and wise words to get you out of trouble. In practicing, take care. Choose a good place with sound anchors and try to operate close to ground level until you become more proficient. Take a course or hire an instructor privately to steer you through the basics and on to more advanced things – it is much less expensive than you might think, particularly if the cost can be spread amongst a group of like-minded people.

During the years since the volumes appearing in this book were first conceived, many people have passed comment and offered ideas on a wide variety of topics associated with ropework for climbing and mountaineering. Often these offerings have proved immensely helpful and I hope that folk will continue to send things from time to time.

Enjoy your climbing!

Nigel Shepherd
North Wales 2001

# A manual of modern rope techniques

for climbers and mountaineers

Nigel Shepherd

Constable London

# Contents

# List of Illustrations

# Acknowledgements

No book of this kind can ever be entirely the work of one person. It must, by its very nature, be a medley of many people's experiences.

To this end I am indebted to lots of people – climbing partners of old and new, novice to superstar – for sharing their experiences and some great days out in the mountains.

In putting this book together I owe a particular debt and I wish to record my thanks.

To Sir Charles Evans for kind permission to quote from his fine book *On Climbing*, still an inspirational instruction book 30 years on. To Martin Atkinson and Mammut for being so generous in supplying equipment for the photographs. To Billy Wayman for some of the best climbing days ever and sharing his extensive technical knowledge. To Brian Hall for reading the manuscript. To Louisa Stieger for helping with the action photos. To Jules and Barbara and Michel at Sport Extreme in Chamonix for the loan of equipment.,

Finally to Helen for lots of things too numerous to mention but mostly for just being there.

This book is for them. Any credit due we shall share but any criticism is entirely my responsibility.

Nigel Shepherd
Chamonix, August 1989

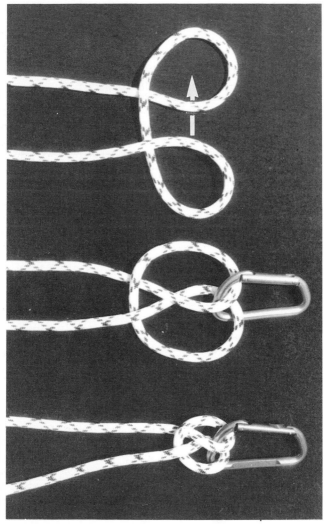

(1) The clove hitch

# Useful Knots and Basic Techniques

This section of the book covers all sorts of basic techniques, knots and methods of tying on to the rope that will be found useful in day to day climbing and mountaineering, and also in the more problematical rescue and self help situations.

In dealing with individual knots or techniques I have treated each in isolation and then made suggestions as to where they might fit in best in the overall rope safety system. By practising each one thoroughly as a separate entity the reader should be able to identify and integrate one or a number of the knots or techniques into his or her day to day climbing and any self-help rescue situation.

As with all knots and techniques there are any number of ways of tying them or putting them into operation. The methods described here are fairly simple and straightforward but once you have mastered the basic skills I'm quite sure you will evolve your own methods of arriving at a safe and correct result.

## THE KNOTS

### Clove Hitch

This knot has been in common usage throughout Europe for a great many years. Its popularity among UK climbers is increasing as people discover its versatility. Form two loops identically as in Photo 1 and pass the right behind the left. With practice the knot can be tied with one hand – useful if you are hanging on for grim death and anxious to arrange an anchor.

There are one or two things that you should be aware of in using this knot. It can be a very difficult knot to undo after it has been subjected to a heavy or continuous loading, particularly in wet ropes or in soft tubular tape. You should also try to avoid tying it in the end of the rope as there may be some slippage. If you do have to tie it in the rope end, make sure that you have plenty of tail end and consider tying off with a couple of hitches or half a double fisherman's (page 25).

*Useful applications*

For tying in directly to anchor points, but only if they are in arm's reach of your stance (see Tying on to Anchors page 114)

Can be used to bring two anchor points to a single point of attachment with a tape or rope sling (Photo 55a)

Tying off pitons on ice or rock

Securing the rope from an anchor point back to the harness

Tying slings or climbing ropes around anchor stakes

## Italian Hitch

A most useful 'sliding friction' knot. Like the clove hitch, it has been in popular usage throughout continental Europe for many years, particularly as a method of safeguarding climbing companions. It is sometimes called a *Munter hitch*.

     To tie this knot, form two loops identically, as in the clove hitch and fold the two together as in Photo 2. It is important that the two loops are formed in the same way otherwise the end result may well be a simple two turns around the karabiner. This will not afford any safety whatsoever. It is best used on a large pear-shaped screwgate karabiner.

     I have often heard it said that this knot causes nylon to rub over nylon so must be unsafe to use. The nylon over nylon danger arises only in situations where a moving nylon rope runs over a static nylon rope. If you study the Italian hitch carefully whilst it is in use, you will see quite clearly that this is not the case. Nylon has a very low melting point, and it is quite possible in situations where a moving rope runs over a static item of kit such as a harness, to generate enough heat to melt the nylon.

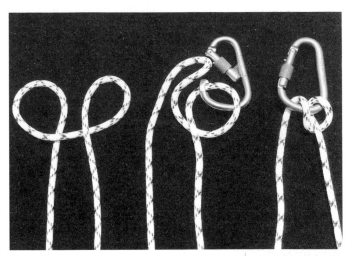

(2a) The Italian hitch

(2b) Tying off an Italian hitch while under load

There are some points to watch out for in use. It twists the rope very badly. Strangely enough some ropes twist more than others, probably due to individual manufacturers' construction designs. This problem can be alleviated to a certain extent by not allowing the rope to twist as it passes through your hand. It is difficult to hold a serious leader fall as the rope slips around the karabiner quite quickly on initial impact. Provided that you can keep a grip on the rope during this early stage a fall is soon arrested. Wearing leather gloves makes it much safer to use. If you are using it as for abseiling on double ropes, it is advisable to treat the two ropes as one and only tie one knot. Using the hitch in narrow karabiners can cause the knot to jam at inconvenient times so it is recommended that you use a large pear-shaped or HMS karabiner. Photo 2b shows how to tie off the hitch under load.

*Useful applications*

As a lowering, abseiling or belaying device

Can be used on a 'direct belay' (page 177)

## Double Fisherman's and Double Fisherman's with Reef Knot

The traditional knot for joining two ends of rope together is the double fisherman's. There is such a thing as a single fisherman's but it is not in common usage nor indeed recommended as it does not have the same holding power. The double fisherman's with reef knot is a good safe knot and is easy to undo after being subjected to a heavy loading, for example when a number of climbers go down the same abseil or when it is necessary to get off the mountain by numerous abseils and the ropes are not untied between each stage. Frequently check the knot for signs of loosening.

When tying the double fisherman's knot you must make

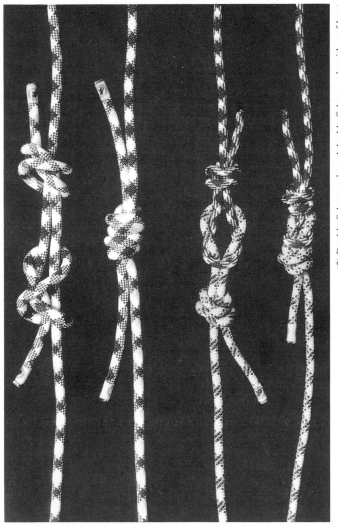

(3) Double fisherman's and double fisherman's with reef knot

(4) The sheet bend

sure that both halves fit snugly into each other. If they don't, the knot is wrong and may come undone when subjected to a severe load (Photo 3).

Whenever you use the knot make sure that there is, at the very least, 4 cm (1½ in) of tail end at each side and that the knot is tied firmly and securely. If you use it to join the ends of rope slung nuts make sure that the knot is well tightened. You should check it frequently for signs of wear and loosening. Do not use it to join two ends of tape together. It is nowhere near as safe or neat as a tape knot.

*Useful applications*

Joining two ropes together on long abseils

Joining the two ends of a rope slung nut

Half a double fisherman's knot is commonly used for tying off the knot that is used to tie into a harness. This is sometimes referred to as a double stopper knot

## Sheet Bend

This knot has very few applications in climbing and mountaineering but is included because it is used in tying the Parisienne baudrier (page 86). It is possible to use it between the double fisherman's knot in place of the reef knot when abseiling. You may also find it useful in self-help situations when you have run out or are short of karabiners. It can be used to connect two slings together but make sure that there is plenty of tail end. It can be used equally well in tape or rope of different diameters but do not mix tape with rope (Photo 4 ).

*Useful applications*

Tying the Parisienne baudrier

Used in a double fisherman's knot instead of a reef knot (see page 22)

## The Tape Knot or Ring Bend

This is the recommended knot for joining two ends of tape together and is most commonly used for making up slings. It is essentially an overhand knot in one end of the length of tape and the other end retraces the line back through the knot to come out on the opposite side (Photo 5). Unlike the fisherman's knot which shouldn't be used in tape, the tape knot can be used in rope. Make sure that the tape lies flat throughout the whole knot and that there is at least 4 cm (1½ in) of tail end. Frequently check any knots tied in thick or 'super blue' tape for signs of loosening. Some people stitch the ends of the knot down but personally I do not recommend this as I have seen the knot move along the sling but still appear to be tied. If used in rope ensure that all the strands lie parallel throughout the knot (Photo 5).

*Useful applications*

Joining two ends of tape together to make a sling

Joining two ends of rope together to make a sling

## KNOTS FOR TYING ON TO THE ROPE.

### The Central Loop

There is a bewildering array of harnesses for climbing available these days. The type of harness that is used most commonly throughout the world is the sit harness – full body harnesses are awkward to handle and constrictive to wear in most mountaineering situations.

The technology and design of sit harnesses has come a long way since the first purpose-made waist belt of some 25 years ago.

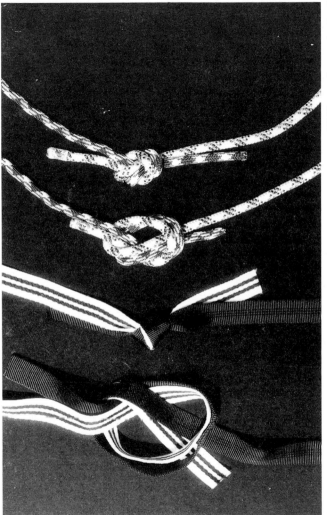

(5) The tape knot or ring bend

All harnesses have specific requirements for tying in to the rope and each individual manufacturer is obliged to provide information on the way in which to tie the rope into a particular harness. You would be well advised to pay close attention to that information as in some cases it may be extremely dangerous to tie in any other way.

In nearly all harnesses there are loops through which the rope should be threaded and these are referred to as the 'tie-on loops'. After threading the rope through these loops a suitable knot is tied to secure the rope to the harness. The loop that is then formed is referred to as the *central loop* and it is crucial to modern rope techniques, particularly those described in this book. Photo 10 shows the loop clearly.

On modern harnesses it plays an important role in attaching belaying devices and for tying on to anchor points. It can also affect the way in which you are able to escape from the system (page 144) and whether or not you are able to do this with your harness intact. The same photo also illustrates how it is used to clip in belay devices and to secure the climber to the anchor point which is, in this case, a clove hitch.

## Bowline

This knot and the figure of eight are without a doubt the most commonly used for tying on to the end of the rope. The bowline is the more traditional, having been used since the early days of mountaineering.

It can be tied into all harnesses with equal security. The basic knot is illustrated in Photos 6a and b. It is important to ensure that the knot is finished off with a half a double fisherman's knot for extra security. This should fit snugly up against the bowline. For further security the knot can be tied with the 'rabbit coming out of two holes' (Photo 6c). This also makes the knot easier to undo after being subjected to a shock load. When tying this knot many people use the 'rabbit out of a hole, around the tree and back in the hole again' technique. It is important to

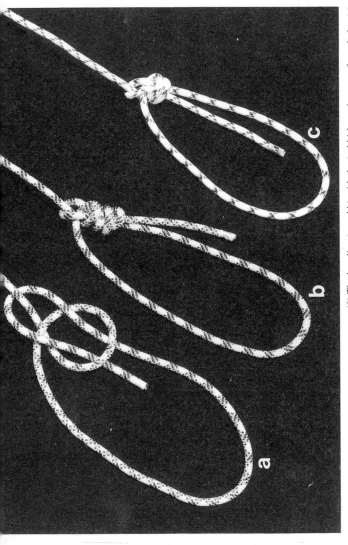

(6) The bowline (a and b) with the 'rabbit' coming out of two holes (c)

ensure that the tree is the main climbing rope in every case.

It can be used to tie the climbing rope directly around the waist. This of course is not as comfortable as a harness but may be necessary from time to time. It will almost certainly cause asphyxiation and death within a short time if you try to hang free with a rope tied directly around the waist.

*Useful applications*

Tying the end of the rope into the harness

Tying the end of the rope around a tree or block or thread anchor

Tying the rope directly around the waist. Only recommended if no harness is available

There are two variations of the bowline that may also be found useful. The first is the bowline on the bight. Photo 7 shows how to tie this knot. Initially it can be a little frustrating to tie but like all knots once mastered it is rarely forgotten. This can be used for connecting a sit harness to a chest harness (page 88) or for bringing two anchor points into one central point. The second variation is the triple bowline (Photo 8). This is essentially used as an improvised body harness. Don't expect it to provide much comfort however!

It is best tied by wrapping the rope around your waist, doubled of course, and then tying a bowline in the normal way but without the double stopper knot to finish it off. Step out of the loop once it is tied. Three loops are formed in doing this and all should be exactly the same size.

To use it as a harness put a leg through a loop each. The third loop goes over your head and one arm. The knot should be at about sternum level.

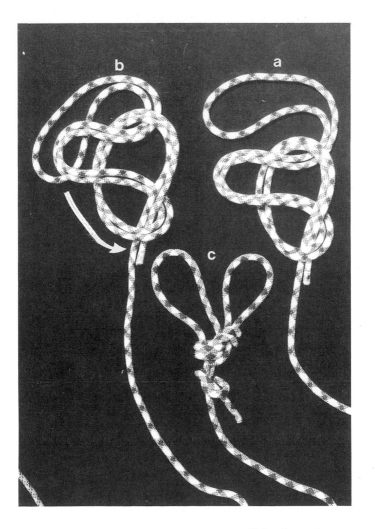

(7) Bowline on the bight

(8) The triple bowline

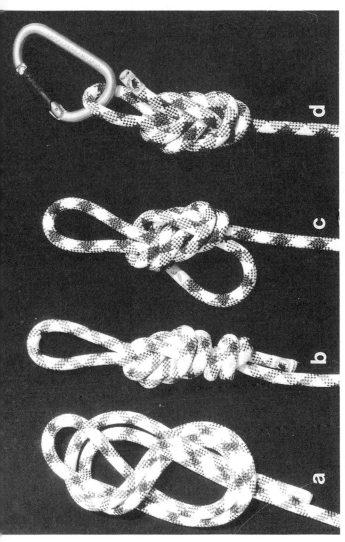

(9) The basic figure of eight knot (a and b) and an alternative method of finishing the knot off (c)

**The Figure of Eight**

This is the other commonly used knot but is slightly more versatile than the bowline as it can be tied in a number of different ways. In its simplest form the figure of eight is tied in a bight of the rope and the finished product provides a loop which can be clipped into a karabiner. This is useful for top-roping or safety-roping situations where the rope is clipped into the harness with a screwgate krab but is generally an inconvenient way of tying in to most harnesses (Photo 9).

There is actually very little that can go wrong when tying the figure of eight but people sometimes end up with an overhand knot or a figure of sixteen or even thirty-two! These are all adequate although the overhand is difficult to undo after loading and the others are just plain cumbersome. A second useful application is for tying in to a harness directly through the manufacturer's recommended tie in loops. Be sure to familiarize yourself with each individual harness tie in method.

When tying the knot directly into the harness the first step is to tie a figure of eight knot in the single rope about 60 cm (2 ft) from the end. The end is then threaded through the tie in loops and the knot completed by tracing the end back through the single figure of eight. Be sure that the ropes going through the knot lie parallel and that the finished loop is neither too small or too large. As a guide to the correct size you should just be able to get your fist through the loop (Photo 10).

The figure of eight can also be used to tie into the middle of the rope. It is not ideal for this purpose – an Alpine butterfly (page 39) is better – but it does suffice. It is tied in a bight of the rope and the loop that is formed can be clipped into a karabiner in the harness. (See Tying into the Middle of the Rope page 184.)

As with the bowline and any other knot in the end of a rope, you should always finish off with the double stopper knot or half a double fisherman's. In most cases this contributes negligibly to the strength of the knot but an enormous amount to the safety of the knot for it ensures that there is enough tail end of rope to

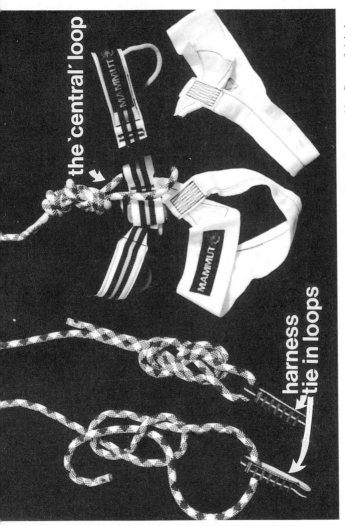

the 'central' loop

harness
tie in loops

(10) Tying the end of the rope into the harness with a figure of eight knot

(11) Figure of eight on the bight

absorb shock without the rope pulling through the knot.

Photo 9c and d shows an alternative way of finishing off the figure of eight knot by tucking the end back into the knot. It is quite popular and uses less rope than a double stopper knot.

Another way in which the figure of eight can be used is in tying back to the harness from an anchor point. This is done using the knot tied in a bight of rope or by threading the doubled rope through the central loop and securing it with a somewhat unwieldy but nevertheless effective knot (see page 115 and Photo 51a). You should be aware that this method is only safe if tied around something of a small diameter, such as illustrated here, the central loop. It would not for instance be as safe to tie it around the harness belt.

The figure of eight, like the bowline, can be tied 'on the bight' that is to say the finished product forms a double loop (Photo 11). This has few applications in climbing other than those already mentioned on page 30 when discussing the bowline on the bight.

*Useful applications*

Tying into the end of rope

Tying back to the harness from an anchor point

Tying in to the middle of the rope

## The Three-Quarters Fisherman

This knot is only included because it is a rather neat way of tying in to the rope end. It is rarely, if ever, used in the UK and the only places I have ever seen it used are the USA and New Zealand. As an addition to your repertoire, however, it is interesting to know and perhaps try.

To begin with you tie an overhand in the single rope about 45 cm (18 in) from the end. Thread the end through the tie in

(12) The three–quarters fisherman's

loops and then pass it through the single knot, finishing off with a double stopper knot or half a double fisherman's (Photo 12).

*Useful applications*

Tying in to rope end

## The Alpine Butterfly

This knot is used for tying into the middle of the rope. It is by far the most suitable knot to use in this situation as it does not put any undue twisting or distorting action on the knot in the event of being subjected to a load. Indeed, it could be said that the knot is designed purely for this purpose.

Although not in common usage, this knot is gaining credence and popularity. I suspect that one of the reasons it has been so ignored over the years is that it is quite complicated to tie (Photos 13a to f). When tying into the middle of the rope one can clip in directly to the loop with a screwgate karabiner. One of the problems, however, with being tied in to the middle of the rope when moving together (page 178) is that one is constantly being pulled from in front or held back from behind. This is particularly awkward for any 'middle people' as they may be on a tricky section of climbing just as the rope becomes tight. Similarly if one member of the party slips there is a chance that they may take the rest with them.

A way around these problems is to tie an Alpine butterfly knot in the rope with a long attachment loop. In the end of the loop you can then tie a figure of eight knot and clip this into your harness. The length of the attachment from harness to Alpine butterfly should be no longer than arm's reach for safety (Photo 14).

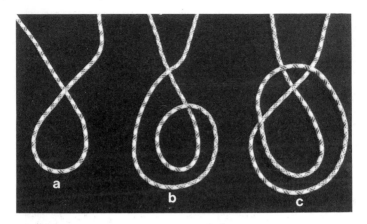

(13) Tying...

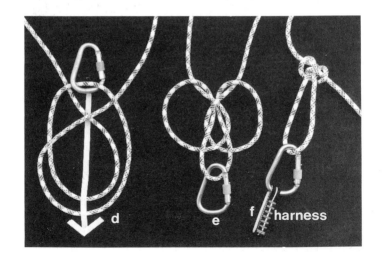

...and finishing off the Alpine butterfly

(14) Attachment to the middle of the rope

(15) The figure of eight with half fisherman's

## The Figure of Eight with Half Fisherman's

Photo 15 clearly shows how this knot is used. A particularly useful application of this knot is in situations where you have a few people to rope up a short section of climbing, on a scramble for instance, and you don't trust the members of your party to tie their own knots correctly.

Tie a figure of eight knot in the single rope then tie a half double fisherman's beyond it. You must make sure that the half fisherman's is finished with the end of rope pointing away from the figure of eight. It is often easier to tie the knot around your own waist first. Once tied, step out of it by sliding the half fisherman's knot away from you. The single figure of eight remains in position. To fit the loop to a smaller person all that is needed is to move the figure of eight away from the half fisherman's. To fit a fatter person move it towards the half fisherman's. When the person steps into the loop, it is a simple matter to tighten it by sliding the two knots together. The two knots must butt up against each other so that when tied around the waist they form a snug but not overly tight or slack loop.

## PRUSIK KNOTS

I use the collective term 'prusik knots' because it is the generally accepted term to describe knots that can be used to ascend a fixed rope – or to descend for that matter. They are also used in self-rescue situations to temporarily secure a rope and some can be used as safety back-up devices or autoblocs (see page 48).

All of the knots described, apart from the Penberthy knot, require a sling of 5 mm (³⁄₁₆ in) or 6 mm (¼ in) cord joined together with a double fisherman's or ring bend. The Penberthy can be used with rope or cord of any diameter provided that the rope that you are tying it to is 9 mm (⅜ in) or thicker. It does not require a closed loop though (page 50). Some of them can be tied with tape slings. For information on the length of loops refer to the section Ascending a Fixed Rope (page 139).

**The Original Prusik Knot**

It is rumoured that this knot was originally invented by a violinist, Dr Karl Prusik, for temporarily repairing violin strings. Quite how true this story is I don't know, suffice to say that it is a useful and well-used knot, and an excellent story!

The basic knot is tied with a loop of thin cord around a thicker rope. The most effective diameter for the loop is 5 mm (³⁄₁₆ in) or 6 mm (¼ in) soft kernmantle. It is quite important to use fairly soft cord as some of the stiffer cords don't grip quite so effectively. It is certainly possible to use thicker cord for the loop but in order to make it work you may have to put in more than the basic two turns around the rope. Remember that each turn you do must go inside the previous one (Photo 16a). It is possible to tie this knot easily with one hand on a taut rope – useful for situations when escaping from the system.

The prusik can cause quite a lot of frustration at times as it tends to tighten up so much in use that it is difficult to release. An effective way to release it after it has been loaded is shown in Photo 16b. Simply roll the loop indicated behind the knot and it will loosen itself. It does not work at all well on wet or icy ropes. On wet ropes it jams severely and on icy ropes it sometimes does not grip at all. Any prusik that tends to slip can be improved by increasing the number of turns around the rope. It must not under any circumstances be used as an autobloc or safety back-up, for once it has been loaded you cannot release it without either cutting it or taking the load off it. It actually works more efficiently on kernmantle ropes if you use hawser laid rope. Number Two nylon is most effective.

In the past people have used the prusik to protect themselves when climbing without a partner. This is done by going around to the top of the cliff and fixing a rope down the intended route. The climber then goes down to the bottom, fixes the other end to an upward-pulling anchor and then attaches on to the rope with a prusik loop. As the climber ascends, the prusik is moved up, thereby affording some security. Whilst it is quite common

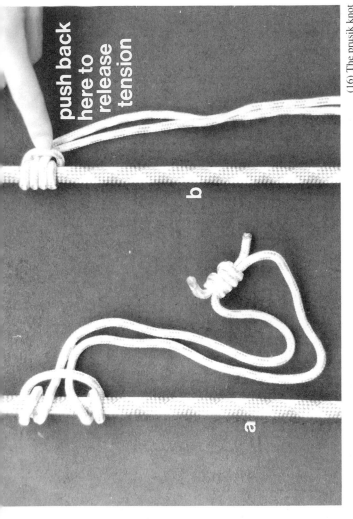

push back
here to
release
tension

b

a

(16) The prusik knot

practice to climb this way you would be advised *never to use a prusik or any other kind of 'prusik' knot for this kind of safety.* Once subjected to a shock loading the loop may well slide down the rope for a short distance and in that movement generate enough heat to melt or fuse it. Either way it is too dangerous to contemplate. A mechanical ascending device is more suited to this task.

It cannot be used effectively when tied in tape.

*Useful applications*

For ascending a fixed rope

Temporarily securing the rope when escaping from the system (page 144)

## The Klemheist

This 'prusik' knot can be tied in cord and has the advantage over the prusik that it can be tied in tape also. In addition, it can be undone more easily after it has been loaded.

Photo 17 shows how to tie the knot. The sling is spiralled around the main rope to create a short loop and a longer loop. It is important that the longer loop is threaded through the shorter loop and the shorter is above the longer. Make sure that all of the turns in the loop lie parallel. Overall it is a much better knot to use than the basic prusik as it causes fewer problems. If using the knot in tape you will find that soft tubular tape works most effectively, though in an emergency the stiffer tapes such as 'Super Blue' work quite well.

You must ensure that the tape lies flat throughout the knot when you tie it. Some distortion always occurs during use but shouldn't cause any problems.

You will find that the Klemheist knot is used quite widely in this book, particularly when we come to discuss glacier travel

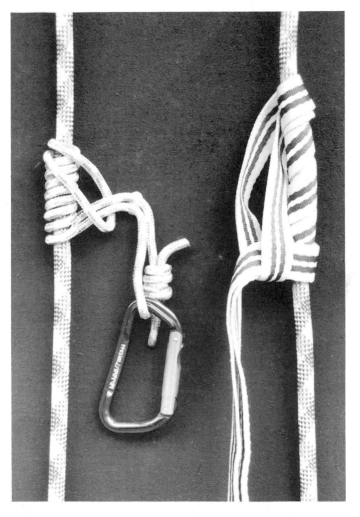

(17) The Klemheist

and crevasse rescue. It is a more efficient alternative to the prusik.

*Useful applications*

Similar to the prusik knot but can also be tied with a tape sling

## The Bachmann

A much used knot but one that I feel has certain limitations. It is effective in use but is prone to distortion and in some cases may prove defective. Its minor disadvantage is that it requires a karabiner – not a problem unless you are short of gear. Photo 18a shows how to tie the knot. The karabiner is often the cause of failure. Its smooth shiny surface comes into contact with the rope so does not actually contribute to the gripping properties of the knot.

It does not work at all on icy ropes!

This is one of a number of knots referred to as *autoblocs*. This means that it is possible to use it in a variety of self-rescue situations as a safety back-up. It will release itself when not under load but lock automatically when a load is applied. Its uses in such situations will be become apparent as you progress through the book.

*Useful applications*

Same as the prusik (page 44)

As an autobloc

## The French Prusik

Of all the 'prusik' knots this is by far and away the most useful. It is sometimes referred to as the 'Johnnyknot' or *the* autobloc. Both terms are incorrect though I'm sure the procurator of the former would be be happy for it to remain as the Johnnyknot. The

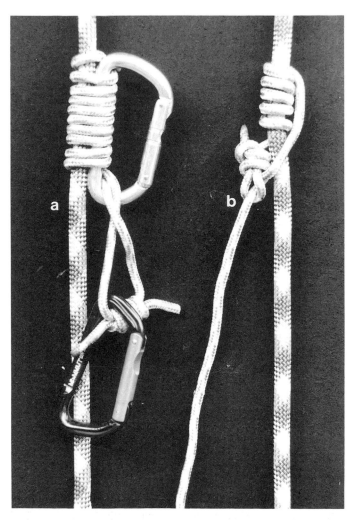

(18) The Bachmann (a) and the Penberthy (b)

latter is incorrect because it is a *an* autobloc. You will find this knot widely used throughout this book. Its prowess in performing many different tasks is unsurpassed by any other knot. Photo 19a shows how the knot is tied.

The best cord to use is 6 mm (¼ in) kernmantle. Make sure that it is good quality and soft as the knot will work even more efficiently. Unlike most of the other prusik knots mentioned this one can easily be released whilst it is under load. For this reason I don't recommend it is used as a knot for ascending the rope. You may inadvertently pull down on it at an inopportune moment and in doing so could cause youself many problems. To release the knot while it is under load all you need to do is pull the knot firmly but smoothly towards the attachment point (Photo 19b). If for some reason it is difficult to release, a sharp jerk should do the trick. Be careful though as the weight is removed quite suddenly.

Always try to clip the two ends of the loop together with a screwgate krab or two snaplinks back to back (Photo 19). There have been circumstances in which the loops have unclipped themselves from a single snaplink.

Do not be tempted to use it as a lowering device, if the rope starts to run you will not be able to stop it without the knot melting under the heat of the friction generated.

*Useful applications*

As an autobloc and safety back-up (page 44)

## Penberthy knot

This knot is included for the main reason that it does not require a loop sling as all the previous knots do. It can be tied in the same diameter cord as the other knots but has the slight disadvantage that it is time-consuming to tie and cannot be done with one hand. Photo 18b shows how the knot is tied. It also works effectively even when tied with 9 mm (⅜ in) rope.

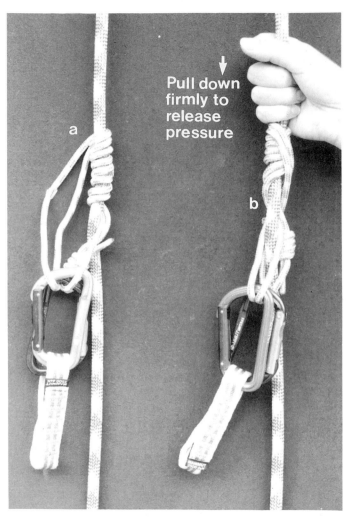

(19) The French prusik

It is one of the few 'prusik' knots that never seems to jam up and that in itself is recommendation enough. However, you will probably find few applications for it in climbing other than in situations where you do not have a 'prusik' loop.

See the final chapter Other Useful Rope 'Tricks' for two applications.

*Useful applications*

When using the retrievable T-axe belay (page 213)

When using the retrievable ice screw (page 215)

## The Alpine Clutch

Though not really a 'prusik' knot of any description, the Alpine clutch is included here because it fits into the family of autoblocs. This is a particularly useful autobloc if you find yourself short of prusik loops. It does however generate a lot of friction and if used in a hoist this often negates some of the mechanical advantage gained in a pulley system.

It works most efficiently on oval shaped karabiners. 'D' shaped krabs not only are less efficient but also jam frequently. If for some reason you do not have oval krabs available try to ensure that you do at least use identical krabs.

To rig the clutch see Photo 20. Clip the rope through both karabiners and decide which is to be the load rope. Take the dead rope, twist it over the load rope karabiner and clip it in. Do not under any circumstances use it as a belaying or abseil device. The rope only moves freely in one direction; it does not move at all in the other.

*Useful applications*

As an alternative autobloc if no prusiks are available

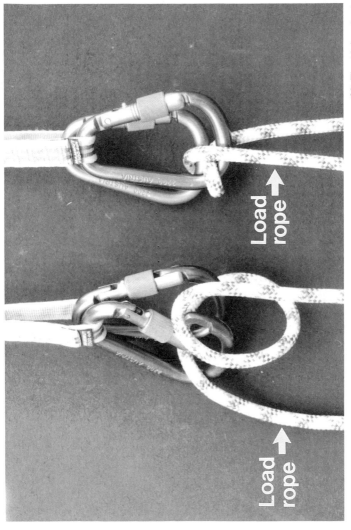

(20) The Alpine clutch

Can also be used for ascending a fixed rope if you only have one prusik loop available (page 143).

## BELAYING

This section covers techniques of belaying – the methods of safeguarding a climber's rope whilst he or she is actually climbing. The term 'belaying' is also commonly used to describe the methods of securing oneself to the mountain. To clarify matters in the text the latter is dealt with under the separate heading Tying on to Anchor Points (page 114).

### The Belay Plate

This is unquestionably the most commonly used method of safeguarding a climber's rope. It is widely used throughout the world and its popularity is well justified for it is a safe and reliable method of belaying. The days of shoulder belays and waist belays are fading fast. Most certainly the former has almost completely disappeared from the scene. These two methods are discussed later.

The belay plate is available in many different styles. There are those that take single 11 mm ($\frac{7}{16}$ in) rope and those that take combinations of sizes of double ropes. Belay plates with two holes, each capable of taking 9 mm ($\frac{3}{8}$ in) or 11 mm ($\frac{7}{16}$ in) ropes are by far the most versatile. Plates with springs are also available. The spring reduces the risk of the plate jamming accidentally during use and serves no other purpose except to ensure the plate gets tangled with all your other gear when not in use.

When you buy a belay plate it is necessary to fix a short loop of cord to it. All plates have the facility for this. The length of the piece of cord that you buy should be about 30 cm (1 ft) long and 4 mm ($\frac{1}{8}$ in) or 5 mm ($\frac{3}{16}$ in) diameter. One end is threaded through a small hole in the plate and tied in an overhand knot. Tie an overhand in the other end and use the loop that is formed to clip into the belay karabiner. This cord helps to keep the

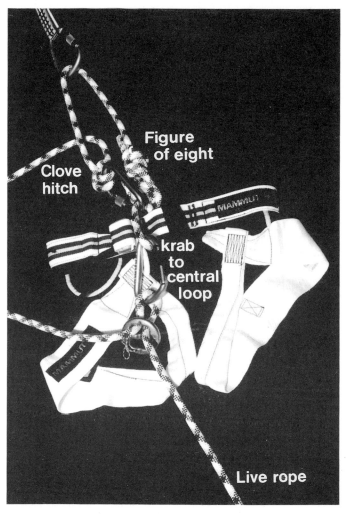

(21) The belay plate

belay plate in place when belaying a second and also secures the plate to yourself to help prevent loss.

You will find that a large pear-shaped or oval screwgate karabiner is most useful in conjunction with a belay plate. It is not necessary to use two karabiners, one for each rope, when using double rope for climbing.

When using the plate in the normal manner it should be clipped into the central loop along with all the other anchor tie offs (Photo 21). You should always ensure that there is enough room for you to be able to lock off the plate if your partner falls. Any small or constricted stances may prove quite awkward in manipulating the plate.

If you are on a hanging stance, that is to say one where there is no ledge to stand on and all the belayer's weight must hang off the anchor points, you may find it awkward to belay someone climbing below you. You will find it easier to operate the plate by clipping the live rope through a krab in the anchor so that your second's rope actually travels up through the anchor and down to your belay plate.

The belay plate can also be used on a 'direct belay'. That is attached directly to the anchor. In such cases it is very important that the plate is operated from behind. In this way you will ensure that it can be locked off correctly. It is not possible to do this when standing in front of the plate. (See direct belaying page 174.)

You may find yourself in the situation where you need to tie off the belay plate. This may happen, for example, when escaping from the system (page 144) whilst there is someone hanging on the end of the rope whose weight makes it difficult to release the plate. In this case you should take the controlling rope (ie the one that locks off the plate) back through the karabiner. You will need to make sure that no rope slips through your hands whilst doing this. Once it is threaded through the krab tie at least two half hitches in front of the plate. This will secure the rope and allow you to use both hands for the next stage of the escape.

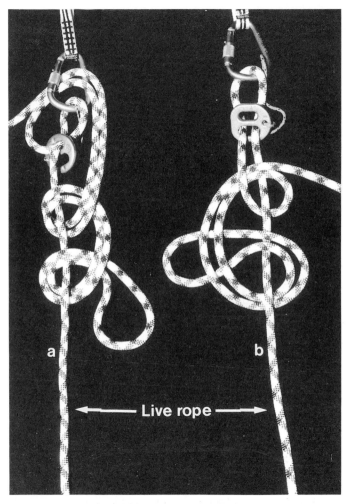

(22) Tying off the belay plate: threading the rope through the krab (a) and tying off in front of the plate (b)

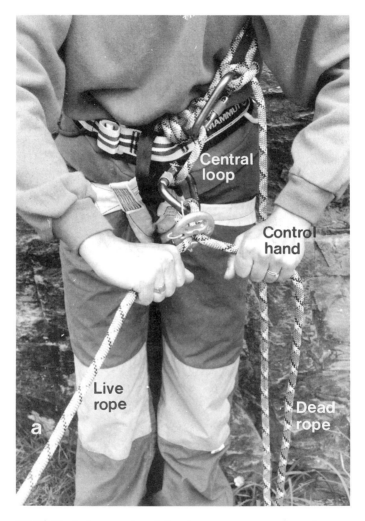

(23a) Taking in the rope using a belay plate – stage one

(23b) Taking in the rope using a belay plate – stage two

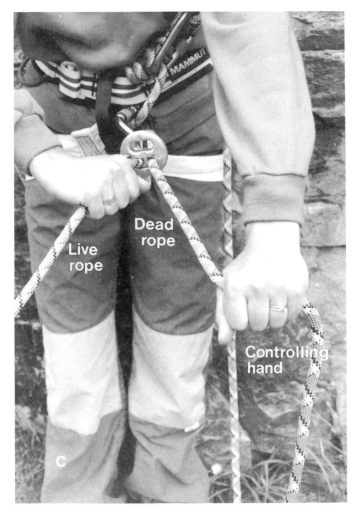

(23c) Taking in the rope using a belay plate – stage three

Tying off the plate in this manner also allows you to untie it whilst it is still under load.

Another way of tying off the plate temporarily is to simply tie a couple of half hitches in front of the plate. This is most useful on a stance where you need to secure your partner whilst gear is sorted out or the guide book consulted. Photo 22 shows both methods clearly.

A third possibility, and one that works better in the latter situation, is to simply tie an overhand knot in the controlling rope. When the knot comes up against the plate it will automatically lock. Do not do this in situations where a load will come on to the plate because unless you are able to take the load off you will not be able to get the knot undone again.

Photos 23a, b and c show the sequence of taking in the rope using a belay plate. This method is applicable to the Lowe belay and figure of eight device mentioned below.

### The Lowe belay tube

The Lowe belay tube comes highly recommended and is a very efficient device, both for belaying and abseiling. Unlike the plate it has much less tendency to twist the ropes and can also be used on quite icy ropes where you may not be able to use a plate. Photo 24 shows how to use the tube in the belay system.

It is normal to use the tube with the wider end facing away from the connecting karabiner. If, however, you need to generate a bit more friction, such as in abseiling, you could use it with the wider end towards the connecting karabiner.

### The Figure of Eight Descendeur

The figure of eight descendeur can also be used as a belaying device. It is less efficient than plates or tubes but nonetheless performs adequately. There are three ways of using it. The first is to set it up exactly as you would for abseiling. Another is to thread the rope through the small hole and use it in the same way

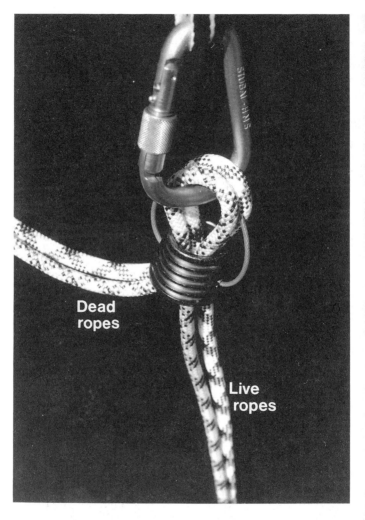

(24) The Lowe belay tube

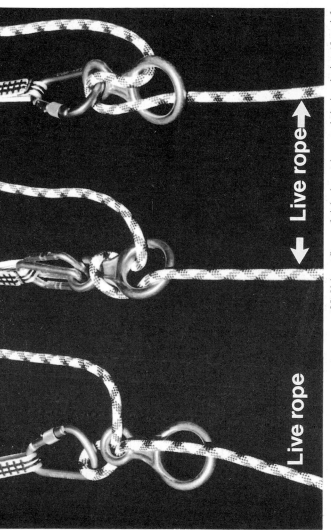

(25) Using a figure of eight descendeur as a belaying device: (*from left to right*) as a plate; the traditional way; using the large hole only

as a plate. The third way is to thread it through the large hole but not through the little hole. Photo 25 shows all three quite clearly.

The problem with the first is that it tends to be awkward to work and twists the ropes. It is also very difficult to operate with double ropes as the individual ropes don't separate easily – paying out or taking in one rope at a time is a problem. If using it as a belay plate it works well but should only really be used with single ropes. The third method of using it works well if it is attached directly to the anchor. It is in common usage on climbs that are well bolted and where the approach is often by abseil so you would carry a figure of eight descendeur in preference to a belay plate. This method works well for bringing up a second but exercise great caution if belaying a leader the same way. You must have upward pulling anchors that are 100% sound.

The figure of eight descendeur is also commonly used when top roping a climber from the ground. It is safer to use it on a direct belay for this purpose rather than attached to the belayer. Be careful if using figure of eight descendeurs as belaying devices when attached directly to the harness. They are particularly awkward to handle.

### The Italian Hitch

The Italian hitch can also be used, though again it makes it awkward to handle double ropes and does of course twist the ropes very badly. When using the hitch always try to use a large pear-shaped karabiner as this eases the problems to a significant extent. See page 20 for relevant notes on the Italian hitch.

### Body Belays

There are two types of body belay: the shoulder belay and the waist belay. The former is almost extinct but is still occasionally used. The latter, though less commonly seen these days, is fairly widely used but by comparison to mechanical methods of belaying they are considered old fashioned.

## The Waist Belay

If you were to show a beginner a body belay and a mechanical belaying device, such as the belay plate, not only would it take them a much shorter time to master the plate, it would also be very much safer to use. Bearing this in mind I consider the waist belay to be a fairly advanced belaying technique and one that in unpractised hands is dangerous.

There are some important considerations to take into account. Firstly, to have any hope of holding a severe fall, gloves must be worn. Long sleeves and good padding around the back are also necessary. This means that on hot, sunny, windless days you can't just wear a T-shirt – unless of course you are happy to run the risk of sustaining terrible rope burns.

Years ago when I worked at Idwal Cottage Youth Hostel, two girls came in early one afternoon and asked if we could be of help. One of the girls had her hands tucked under her armpits, the other could barely walk. As the tale unfolded we discovered that they had decided to 'have a go' at rock climbing and acquired a rope, but no other gear. They spotted some people climbing on the Gribin Facet, though of course they didn't know its name, and thought they'd go up there. The first girl, the one with her hands in her armpits, had climbed up, sat on the top and told her friend to follow. Unfortunately near the top her friend fell and she was unable to stop the rope from sliding through her hands. Her friend tumbled all the way to the bottom of the cliff, but not too fast because she held on to the rope all the way. It is sufficient to say that the rope burns were pretty horrible.

Secondly, you should always bring the rope over your head when putting it around your waist. 'Stepping' into it often leads to tangles and if you fail to hold a falling second the rope can be pulled down around your knees. By looping it over your head the ropes to the anchor prevent it sliding down below your waist.

When operating the waist belay you will have a 'live' rope and a 'dead' or 'controlling' rope. The live rope has the other climber directly on the end of it and the dead rope goes to the pile of slack rope you have beside you.

Always twist the dead rope around the arm that holds it and under no circumstances let go of it. *Never* twist the live rope around your arm – any sudden load may snap your arm.

If you are tied to an anchor point via the front of your harness, make sure that the live rope comes around on the same side as the rope from the anchor. Photos 26a, b and c show the technique for taking in the rope safely. Any loading will then twist you into the anchor rather than out of it which may cause you to let go of the rope.

When belaying the leader always arrange your stance so that if the person falls they do not fall in such a way that the rope comes away from your waist. This means that if you are facing into the crag you must make sure that the live rope comes out on the opposite side of your body that the load is likely to come from. If you are facing out from the crag, the live rope must come around on the same side that you anticipate the load to come from and twist your body slightly towards that side. For extra safety the live rope could be clipped into a karabiner on a strong point of the harness somewhere near the central loop. Always make sure that you have sufficient space to be able to lock off the rope in the correct manner for holding a fall.

If you have to escape from the system (page 144) when using the waist belay, you can release both hands if you wrap the controlling rope repeatedly around your leg and finally stand on it to trap it. This is terribly uncomfortable so make sure that you work quickly!

*The Shoulder Belay*

This method of body belaying, illustrated in Photo 27 is most useful for hauling people up climbs and for quick belays when moving together. It is important that it is set up as illustrated, with the live rope coming from underneath the armpit. If it comes over

(26a) Taking in the rope using a waist belay – stage one

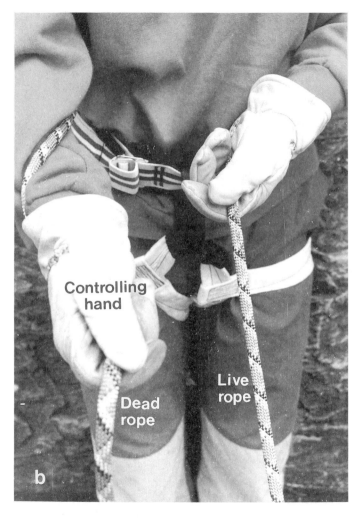

(26b) Taking in the rope using a waist belay – stage two

(26c) Taking in the rope using a waist belay – stage three
Then return to (a) and repeat the sequence

(27) The shoulder belay

your shoulder any loading on it will tip you forward and may pull the rope off. You need to be well braced, preferably leaning against the rock, with the leg on the same side as the live rope braced slightly forward. You *must not* use this method for belaying a leader.

## LOWERING

Most of the times you go down on a rope will either be by climbing down or by abseil. There could, however, be the odd occasion where you need to be lowered down by your partner. Such an occasion could be as part of a rescue or perhaps when you are descending but are a little unsure of what lies ahead. If you are being lowered you can go down to see what's ahead and, should you discover that the route is impassable your partner can belay you while you climb back up without having to change the belay system at all.

The device that you use for lowering could be a figure of eight, a belay plate, karabiner brake, Italian hitch or any other suitable method. For notes on these please refer to the appropriate part of the book.

Whichever device or knot you choose to use, it is worth putting on a French prusik safety back-up. This is attached to the live rope and thence to the anchor. Putting this on allows you to rest and take both hands off the controlling rope if you need to, though if you intend leaving the lower for some time you should tie the device off by an appropriate method (Photo 28).

To convert a lower into a belay to bring a climber back up as in the situation quoted, all you need to do is pull the rope through the lowering device instead of letting it out. You don't even need to take the French prusik safety back-up off.

### Passing a Knot

If, on a rescue for example, you need to join two ropes together you can pass the knot through a lowering device fairly simply.

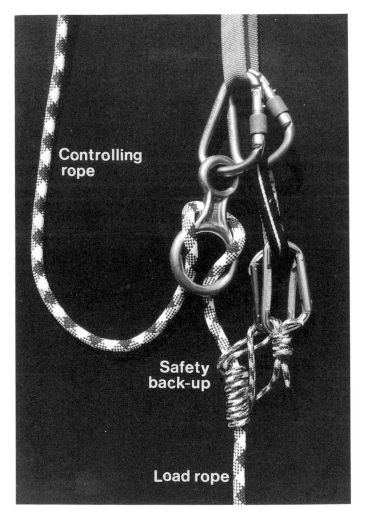

(28) The French prusik being used as a safety back–up on a lower

The technique for this is essentially the same as that described for abseiling past a knot (page 135 and Photo 61). With the safety back-up already on, allow the joining knot to come about 30 cm (1 ft) from the lowering device. This must coincide with all the load coming on to the safety back up. Take the rope out of the device and put the rope back in with the knot below and having theoretically passed through the device. Make sure that the knot is hard up against the device and gradually lower the load back on by gently releasing the autobloc a little at a time. Once the load is back on, release the autobloc to allow the knot to pass by and then put it back on again. Make sure that the autobloc is long enough to allow the load to come back on to the device after passing the knot.

Another method of passing the knot is illustrated in Photos 29a and b. The system is identical to that previously described except that a Mariner's knot and prusik is used in place of the French prusik. Allow the joining knot to come 30 cm (1 ft) from the lowering device, put on the prusik and then tie the Mariner's knot, take the load on the prusik, pass the knot and gradually release the Mariner by allowing it to untwist itself slowly. Please note that for the Mariner's knot to work efficiently you must have quite a long prusik loop.

## Cowstail

A cowstail is a short attachment from the harness that can be used to clip into an anchor point without having to use the rope to tie in. It must be attached to a part of the harness that will safely support your weight without relying on the rope.

It is possible to buy pre-stitched slings that have a number of different loops to which you can attach yourself. These are sometimes called 'snake' slings. An item of equipment such as this is indispensable in self-rescue situations. If however, you are not so fortunate to own a snake sling, one can easily be improvised from a tape sling or quick draws.

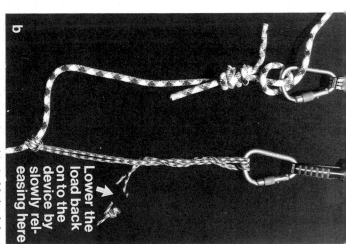

**Lower the load back on to the device by slowly rel-easing here**

(29) Passing a knot through a lowering device using the Mariner's knot

(30) A larksfoot

## Larksfoot

This is the term used to describe a method of securing a sling to an anchor (Photo 30). It is quick and convenient to do but in some instances, such as extending wire runners, it is very dangerous to use. I include it here because I mention its use in other situations later in this book. It is most useful when ascending a fixed rope or 'prusiking' (page 139) to secure the foot loop.

## THE HANGING HOIST

This technique, as with many others in the book, is described as an individual exercise that forms a part of a larger operation. If you have a victim who is hanging on the end of a rope and you wish to release the rope from their harness, you have a number of options.

The first option to consider is to get the victim to stand on a ledge or foothold nearby and take enough weight off the rope to allow you to untie it. *Remember* though that you should attach the victim into the new rope or anchor point before untying the original rope.

If the victim is unable to help you in any way or is hanging free, the second option, having already clipped the victim into the new tie-on or anchor, is to simply cut the rope near the original tie-on. Be very careful if you choose this option, for two reasons. Firstly, there will be a lot of ropes and general mêlée around you and the victim so be sure that you cut the right rope. Secondly, when a rope is under tension a sharp knife will cut it cleanly and surprisingly easily, so be careful not to slip with the knife and cut other ropes as well.

The third option available to you is more complicated than the previous two, but is the one you are most likely to have to use. Photo 31 shows the basic set-up for this technique. Proceed as follows: abseil down until your feet are level with the victim's chest and lock off so you don't go any further. Put a prusik loop (a short one) on the victim's rope and clip in a krab. Pass a long

(31) The hanging hoist

sling through the krab and clip one end of it to the victim's
harness – *not* into the central loop. If you put your foot into the
other end of the sling and pull the victim up with your arms, at
the same time pushing down hard with your leg, the victim will
move up surprisingly easily and their weight will come off the
end of the rope. You must find some way to keep the victim's
weight off the old end of rope whilst you untie it. This could be
done by putting a French prusik on the victim's new rope (which
will already be tied in) and attaching it to another prusik on your
own rope or fixing it to your person. This temporarily holds the
victim whilst you untie the old rope and you can then lower him
or her on to the new rope by releasing the French prusik.
Alternatively, if you have an assistant at the top of the new rope
they can take in the rope tightly as you effect the hanging hoist
and when you release the load from the foot sling the victim
drops on to the new rope.

  *Remember* that whichever option you choose you must
always attach the victim to the new rope or anchor before untying
the original rope.

## COILING THE ROPE

The 'traditional' way of coiling a rope is illustrated in Photos 32.
Unfortunately most modern ropes do not comply very well with
this method. Unless you deliberately try to take the twists out of
the rope it will not lie flat and neatly coiled as illustrated.
However, forcing the twists out of the rope can do harm to the
long-term durability and handling properties of the rope. It is
much better to allow the rope to twist as it wants to than to make
it do something that's not good for it. A better method is
illustrated in Photos 33. This is known as 'lap coiling' and it is
much better for the rope. The sequence shows how to coil a rope
this way and how to finish the coiling off. The spare rope left
after coiling can be used to tie the rope to your back, leaving your
hands free to hold on to the rock.

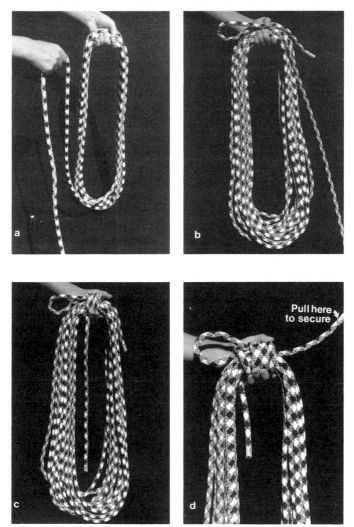

(32) Coiling a rope in the traditional way

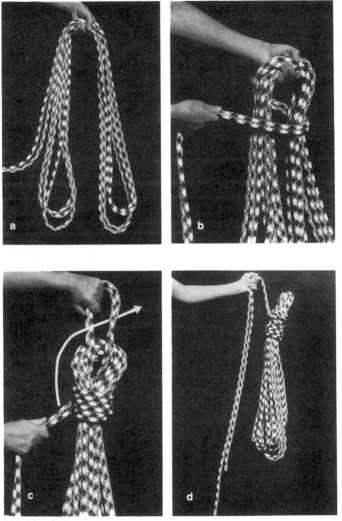

(33) Lap coiling

## IMPROVISED HARNESSES

The vast majority of modern-day climbers use a purpose-made harness of one kind or another: a sit harness, simple waist belt or full body harness. Nevertheless, you may find yourself in a situation one day that requires an improvised harness. A typical example is if you are climbing with a party that only have waist belts and you decide to do a bit of abseiling with them. Another occasion might be in glacier travel when you only have a sit harness and feel a chest harness combined with a sit harness would be safer.

It is well worth bringing to your attention here that it is not possible for anyone to hang on the end of a rope by the waist for more than a few minutes without causing great discomfort, asphyxiation after about ten minutes and death within twenty minutes. You should, therefore, never lower or abseil off a direct waist tie.

A simple method of relieving the weight off a waist tie is to clip a long sling on to the main climbing rope with a karabiner, slide it down until it is up against the waist tie and stand in it. This is of course only a temporary solution to the problem and a more comfortable harness should be rigged as soon as possible.

### Sit Slings

The Dulfer seat is probably the most commonly used improvised sit sling. It requires a 2.4 m (8 ft) sling for the average-sized person.

Pass the sling behind the back but do not step into it at all. The knot or sewn join should be positioned in the middle of the back. Pull a loop either side of your body and one up between your legs. Clip all three loops together at the front with a large screwgate karabiner (Photo 34a). For extra security the three loops could be clipped into the waist tie or belt. On small people the tape can be tucked up through the waist belt and turned around a few times to take up the slack. There is no safety or

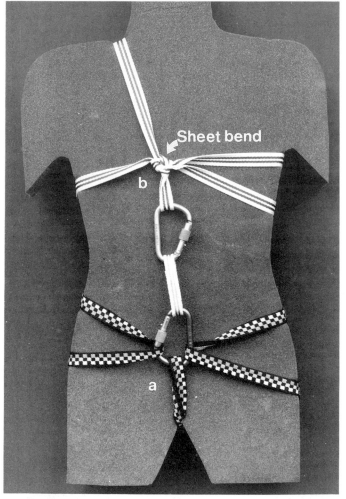

(34) A Dulfer seat (a) and Parisienne baudrier (b) connected
to make an improvised full body harness

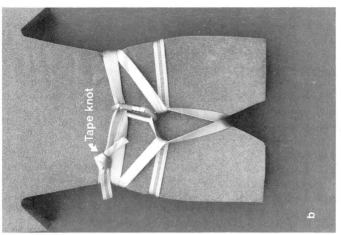

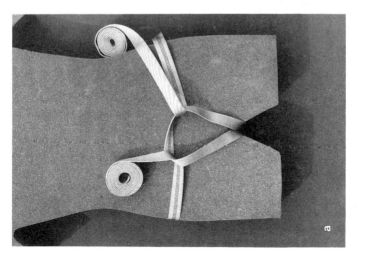

(35) An improvised sit harness made from a 4 m length of tape

comfort in a Dulfer sling that is continually falling around the knees.

If for some reason your sling is not long enough to go around the person, a simple and effective sit sling can be arranged by twisting the sling once to form a figure of eight. Step one leg into each loop and bring the centre up to clip into the waist belt or tie. Any slack can be taken up and tied in a knot on one side.

The Dulfer seat is really only of use provided that it is under constant tension. It's not worth using it as an alternative to a proper sit harness for general mountaineering. It slips down around the legs and is generally very awkward. An interesting and more comfortable, longer lasting sit harness can be constructed with a 4–4.5 m (13–14½ ft) length of tape. The wider the tape the more comfortable the harness. Photos 35a and b show how to rig this up. The ends are joined together using the tape knot. Whilst it is longer lasting than the Dulfer it is not comfortable to hang in for a long time as the leg loops squeeze and cut into the thighs.

A third improvisation is illustrated in Photo 36. This requires two short slings (120 cm (4 ft)). Tie an overhand knot about two-thirds of the way along each sling and step one leg into each of the larger loops. Thread the waist belt through the two shorter loops of the slings or clip them to a krab on the belt and make sure that when you tie on you thread the rope through both slings and the waist belt. If you do not have a waist belt you could use a third sling around the waist instead or even the end of the rope.

## Chest Harnesses

In Britain climbers rarely have cause to resort to wearing a chest harness. Perhaps the only time that you would certainly use one is in an emergency situation involving the lowering of a victim (see Assisted Evacuation page 164). In such cases a chest harness makes it more comfortable for the victim and indeed may also make it more comfortable for the rescuer.

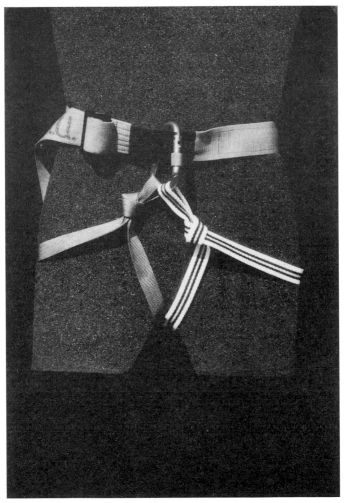

(36) A sit harness made from two short slings
connected to the waist belt for security

In Alpine regions, however, where a fall into a crevasse may result in a climber hanging free, some kind of chest support is essential. The reasons for this are quite simple – the centre of gravity of the human frame is at the sternum and wearing a rucksack makes the body top-heavy. The more weight in a rucksack the more top-heavy the climber is. The attachment point of a sit harness is very much lower than the centre of gravity so that in a fall into space, particularly, the climber is likely to tip upside down and may even fall out of the harness. There are ways of gaining chest support by the manner in which the rope is tied to the climber (see Moving Together page 184). However satisfactory these methods may seem, they are never as convenient as a properly rigged chest harness, improvised or otherwise.

*Parisienne Baudrier*

The simplest but most effective chest harness to improvise is the Parisienne baudrier. It requires a 2.4 m (8 ft) sling of at least 2.5 cm (1 in) wide tape. If you are able to get 5 cm tape the overall harness will be more comfortable to wear.

To tie the harness, pass one arm through the sling and bring the rest of the sling under the opposite armpit. Tie a sheet bend in the manner illustrated in Photo 4. It is very important to ensure that you *do not* pass the end of the sling through the loop that goes over the shoulder. If you do the resulting knot will be a slip knot and any load will only tighten the sling around the body causing eventual asphyxiation and possibly death. The harness should be snug but not tight enough to cause restricted movement. After tying the knot there should be at least a large enough loop to clip a karabiner in (Photo 34b).

To be absolutely truthful, there are few other improvised chest harnesses that are as effective. Crossed sling baudriers and others that may have been suggested in the past make poor and dangerous alternatives.

The most likely problem that you will encounter with the

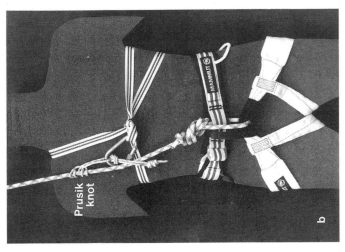

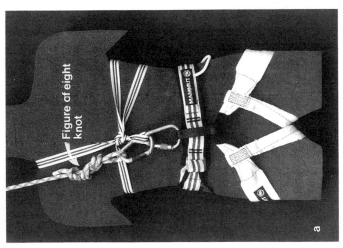

(37) Two ways of connecting a sit harness to an improvised chest harness

Parisienne baudrier is that the sling may not be long enough to go around the chest. It is a simple matter to rectify this by adding another shorter sling on to the part of the sling that comes under the armpit. This will allow extra tape for tying the sheet bend.

## Improvised Body Harness

The Dulfer seat or any of the other improvised sit harnesses and Parisienne baudrier can be connected together to make a full body harness. There are a number of ways of doing this, the choice of method depending on the situation you find yourself in and the equipment available to you. If you have a long enough loop after tying the sheet bend on the Parisienne baudrier, clip the loop into the Dulfer seat karabiner thus connecting the two together. Photos 37a and b show ways to connect a purpose-made sit harness to an improvised chest harness and two different methods of attaching the rope. Similar methods can be employed for an improvised sit harness.

## DOUBLE ROPE TECHNIQUE

The use of two ropes in most climbing scenarios allows greater flexibility in the protection of both leader and second, and also in dealing with emergencies or retreating from the mountain. Whilst tangles inevitably occur (no matter how experienced the climbers), by adopting a fairly logical and thoughtful approach such annoyances can be kept to a minimum.

The choice of diameter of rope must be left to the individual. Sometimes two 8.8 mm ($\frac{5}{16}$ in) ropes, or even thinner, may be sufficient. At other times combinations of thick and thin may fit the bill. Rarely, however, will two 11 mm ($\frac{7}{16}$ in) ropes be necessary. Remember that there are certain standards and recommendations made by the international safety body, the UIAA, concerning the different uses to which a rope may be put.

When using double ropes for climbing, try to make sure that you begin the day with the ropes free of any tangles, twists or kinks. When placing running belays on a climb, try to keep one rope for runners to your left and the other for runners to your right. Often this will mean looking carefully at the route prior to setting off and doing a bit of careful planning. On stances, try to run both ropes through to check for tangles before setting off again. Run them through individually if possible.

When using a belay plate to safeguard another climber, both ropes can be clipped into the same karabiner. Attaching to multiple anchor points is very much simpler – use one rope for each anchor.

# Snow, Rock and Ice Anchors

In this chapter I propose to discuss mainly the methods that can be employed to tie on to various types of anchor. It is not really within the remit of this book to discuss at length the methods of placement of anchors; however I think that there are one or two aspects that merit discussion.

## ANCHORS ON ROCK

Anchors on or in rock can be fashioned many different ways. From simple slings to bolts; from Friends to nuts; from pitons to trees. Anything that is secure enough to hold the party to the mountain will suffice, provided that it is ethically acceptable of course.

However, when you create an anchor on rock, or snow and ice for that matter, consider firstly what you require of that anchor. It goes without saying that it must be able to hold everyone to the mountain, but consider also the direction that the load may be coming from. A sling draped over a small spike at your feet will not hold an upward pulling force such as that experienced when holding a leader fall. Consider also how much force you expect to come on to an anchor. It's no good expecting an RP size 0 to hold the weight of two climbers during an assisted evacuation. So often accidents occur as a result of the party having paid little attention to their own safety when rigging up anchors. Tragically, some end in death.

### Nuts or Chocks

These come in an enormous variety of shapes and sizes these days – too many to mention individually.

When placing any nut in a crack, do so with careful thought. It's all very well to say that here of course – when you're hanging on by fingertips halfway up an overhanging wall somewhere, it's a whole different ball game. Make sure that there is plenty of

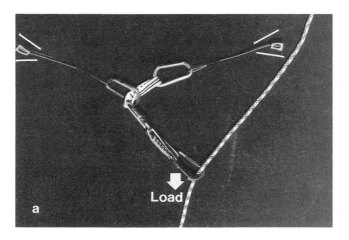

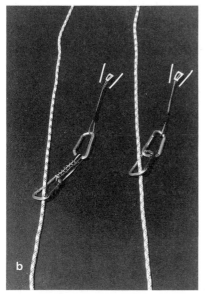

(38) Nuts placed in opposition to each other (a). Such a set-up is not safe unless both nuts are well placed. The correct way to extend wire runners (b)

rock around the nut so that any load will tighten it in to the crack. Make sure too that extracting it will be a simple matter. When used as running belays you will also have to make sure that they are well seated so that the rope running through a karabiner does not lift the nut out.

Any small nuts should ideally be threaded with wire. Any nuts that take cord thinner than 7 mm (¼ in) will be considerably less strong than the same nut threaded with wire. Wire nuts will often need to be extended to reduce leverage and the possibility that they might come out at an inopportune moment. Always extend wire runners by connecting the extension to the wire with a karabiner. Connecting with a sling directly around the wire is unacceptably dangerous (Photo 38b). You may of course have to extend any running belay from time to time and the same theory applies.

Nuts in opposition to each other can sometimes provide a satisfactory anchor or runner where otherwise you would have nothing. When rigging such an anchor you must be absolutely certain that the forces involved in loading will not pull the nuts out of the crack (Photo 38a). If one nut fails, the other is almost certain to fail too.

Nut placement is something of a science, study it carefully and learn well.

## Slings

To use a sling is one of the oldest methods of anchoring used in climbing. It is well worth considering buying pre-stitched slings. They are much more convenient than the knotted variety. Unlike a knot the stitching cannot work loose or slip through itself. However there may be the odd occasion where a knotted sling would be of use and it is certainly worth carrying a couple when mountaineering.

Slings come in a variety of sizes from quick draws through to 2.4 m (8 ft) slings and from lightweight tubular tape to heavier super tape. Slings can also be made out of rope,

(39a) A sling stretched too tightly over a block

(39b) A much safer anchor

though they are seen much less commonly these days. There are a few special considerations to take into account. The most important one worth mentioning is that if using a sling draped over a spike or flake or threaded around a rock or tree, you must make sure that it is not stretched too tightly around the object. A sling placed such is considerably weaker than one that has some slack in it (Photos 39a and b). Make sure that there are no sharp edges to cut into the material.

## Friends

The invention of Friends and, more recently, other devices along the same lines has revolutionized protection for climbers. A well-placed Friend is as strong and reliable as a well placed nut or sling around a spike. Like all gear they take a bit of practice to get used to. Take care not to cram the cams into a crack as they can be difficult, if not impossible, to remove.

## Pitons

Pitons are not commonly used in the UK these days. The old expression 'that a man who would use a piton on British rock would shoot foxes' has kept their use to a minimum. However, they are in popular usage in winter climbing and in Alpine mountaineering.

One would most commonly encounter a piton in an 'in situ' position on the mountain. If that be the case you must establish that it looks strong enough to be used safely. Sometimes pitons have been in situ for a good many years and though they may appear outwardly strong, underneath all sorts of corrosion may have taken place. Some years ago I was climbing the East Wall Girdle on the side of the Idwal Slabs. On that route there was a semi-hanging belay, the main anchor being an in situ piton. There was already a climber on the stance and so there was no room for me. After a short wait he began to vacate the stance and I moved into position. I thought that it would be prudent to check out the piton anchor so put in a sling and krab and pulled on it pretty violently. The head snapped off completely. The previous incumbents of the stance had been tied solely to that piton.

When placing pitons choose a crack into which at least the first quarter of the piton can be placed by hand. Having done that, hammer it in until it makes a high ringing sound. Any placement that makes a dull thudding sound is usually less secure and a fatter but shorter peg may be needed. If the piton reaches a point where it refuses to go any further, do not persist in hammering it to death but tie it off in a similar manner to that illustrated in Photo 49b page 112. Make sure that you tie it off as close to the rock as possible to reduce the leverage.

## ANCHORS ON SNOW

Generally speaking always try to use rock anchors as they are much more reliable. There will, however, be occasions when it simply will not be possible to select a rock anchor. In such cases a variety of snow anchors are available. On a cautionary note you should remember that snow is not as predictable in quality as rock. A seemingly sound anchor may well fail when put to the test. Having said that, if you are able to arrange an anchor in good compact snow and it is set up correctly, there is no reason why it shouldn't hold a substantial load.

### Ice Axe Anchor

In its simplest form an ice axe anchor can be arranged by driving the axe vertically into the snow. It is necessary to have a consistently sound snow pack for this to work efficiently. There should not be any weak underlying layers in the snow which may cause failure under load. Occasionally it may not be possible to get the ice axe the whole length of the shaft, in which case it should be tied off at the snow to reduce leverage.

If the snow is not so compact it may be better to use a buried ice axe anchor. The horizontally buried axe illustrated in Photo

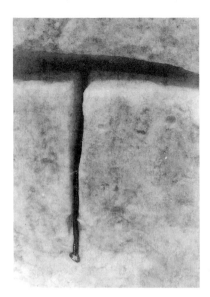

(40) A horizontally buried ice
axe in a T-slot *left*.
Detail of the horizontally
buried axe *below*.
The sling is clove hitched
around the shaft

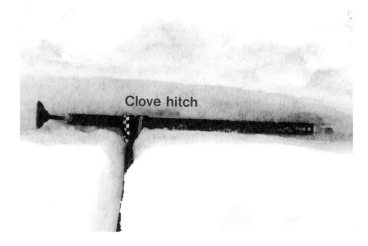

Clove hitch

40 makes a fairly effective anchor in reasonably compact snow. It is necessary to cut down fairly deeply into the snow pack and to cut a small trench to accommodate the sling attachment point. When you are cutting out the slot for the axe take great care not to disturb the snow in front of the anchor. This is integral to the reliability of the anchor.

When you attach a sling to the shaft of the ice axe, do so before you put the axe in and attach it about two-thirds of the way along from the spike to the head and make sure you place the pick down into the snow.

Photo 41a shows a much stronger method of making an anchor but it is of course one that requires two axes. This method is called the T-axe for obvious reasons. Having cut out the slot for your horizontal axe (still bearing in mind the above considerations), you simply take the second ice axe and drive it in slightly back from the vertical, behind the horizontal axe. The sling should go on first of course and should be clove hitched around the shaft. Ideally the vertical axe should be driven right to the head but if this is not possible it can be tied off at the level of the horizontal axe. The sling should come over the top of the horizontal axe so that any loading helps to hold it in place.

Various combinations, such as the horizontal behind the vertical, are possible (Photo 41b). Note that in all cases the vertical axe is placed close to the head of the horizontal axe rather than centrally.

If you are using two tools and one is shorter than the other it is generally better to place the shorter one as the horizontal axe.

Once the anchor is set up and in position it is sometimes necessary to fill in the slot with snow and stamp it down firmly to make sure that the gear remains buried.

A large stance should be cut downhill of the anchor and you must sit down to belay. You may have to get well below the anchor for it to work effectively.

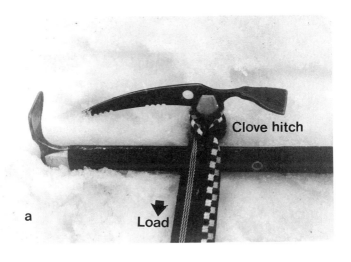

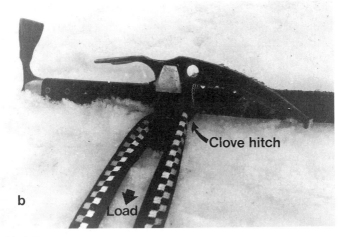

(41) A T-axe anchor with a vertical axe behind (a) and a T-axe anchor with vertical axe in front (b). In both cases the sling is attached to the rear axe

## Other Buried Items!

It is possible to secure yourself to almost anything buried in a slot or trench in the snow. Though highly unlikely I have heard people say that it is possible to anchor to a buried glove! A rucksack is certainly a feasible option. Make sure that you take out any gear that you need before you bury it though. A sling can be clove hitched around the body of the sack and to create extra length additional slings can be added. The sling is then run out of the T-slot and you attach yourself to this point. As with buried axes be careful not to disturb the snow in front of the slot. You should also stomp some snow over the top and bury the rucksack completely.

## The Deadman Anchor

The Deadman is a spade-shaped plate made of alloy and has a wire fixing to which all anchor attachments are made. A smaller version, the Deadboy, is available. It is a popular type of snow anchor among British climbers but not so throughout the rest of the world. Placed correctly they provide solid, reliable anchors. Unfortunately, placement is so critical that they often fail under the lightest of loadings. In addition they are the most awkward item of climbing equipment to carry that has ever been invented.

To place the Deadman as an anchor you should proceed as follows. Cut a slot across the slope; this should be quite deep, depending on the quality of snow. The poorer the snow, the deeper the slot. You must now cut a second slot down the hill at 90 degrees to the first. This is to accommodate the wire strop.

Take an imaginary line at 90 degrees to the angle of the slope and bisect it with the Deadman. Tilt the Deadman a little closer to the upper slope and then hammer it into the snow until it is at least 30 cm (1 ft) below the bottom of the trench. It is important that you maintain the angle of 40 degrees as you hammer it in. Any other angle may cause the anchor to fail under load.

Once in position you must tie yourself into the strop. Any of the methods described in Tying on to Anchors (page 114) is suitable. You must, however, remember to stay well below the slot that the Deadman was placed in originally. This may mean that you have to go down the hill for 3 (12 ft) or even 5 m (20 ft). The reason for this is that the angle between the wire and the plate should not exceed 50 degrees. You should cut out a deep hole and sit in it to belay. Make sure that you also have something to brace your feet against.

It is hardly surprising when you consider all the critical factors of placement, that the Deadman plate is not popular.

## Snow Stake

A method of fashioning an anchor in snow that is used widely in New Zealand. It is becoming more common worldwide now. Basically this is a piece of 'angle iron' but made of alloy and with a point at one end and holes for attachment at the other. The stake is driven slightly back from the vertical with the point of the 'V' shape facing the direction of pull. It can also be placed horizontally in a T-slot.

## The Snow Bollard

Surprisingly enough, the snow bollard can be a very effective anchor. They are most commonly used as abseil anchors in situations where there is nothing else available and you wish to leave no equipment behind. They can be used equally well of course, as anchors from which to belay (Photo 42).

The snow bollard is prepared by cutting a teardrop shape in the snow with the point of the teardrop pointing towards where the load is expected to come from. The trench that is cut around the shape should be cut much deeper at the top than at the bottom. It should also be undercut slightly to enable the rope to sit more securely. The widest diameter of the bollard is determined by the quality of the snow that it is cut into. Basically the poorer the quality of snow, the wider the bollard.

(42) A snow bollard. Note that the anchor has been reinforced with an ice axe and that the belayer sits well below the anchor

(43) Abseiling over a bergschrund. A bollard was used as an anchor

The rope, when placed around the bollard, tends to work a bit like a cheese wire and if the snow is not especially solid it will quite simply pull through. To alleviate the problem slightly, the back of the bollard can be padded with a rucksack, ice axe or, if you are using it to retreat from, anything that you are prepared to leave behind. If you do have to use a very large snow bollard to retreat from, you will probably find that the amount of friction generated by the rope is enough to prevent you from being able to recover the ropes after abseiling. To alleviate the problem to a certain extent, quickly see-saw the rope back and forth around the bollard just before you set off. This creates an icy groove which the rope will slide into more easily.

You will almost always have to use the rope directly around the anchor to secure yourself, so use any of the methods appropriate in the section Tying on to Anchors (page 114). As with the Deadman you must cut your stance well below the anchor and sit down to belay.

## Foot Belays

These techniques are particularly effective for safeguarding someone climbing up from below or someone descending. They can also be usefully employed in glacier travel for safeguarding someone who is making an exploratory manoeuvre among crevasses.

The New Zealand boot axe belay is effective in good hard snow. Photo 44 shows the technique being used. Note that the pick of the axe points forward and one hand remains pushing it into the snow. Friction, which enables you to take the strain, is generated by increasing the amount of rope in contact with the ankle. Do not be tempted to wrap the rope around the ankle to increase the friction. Some weight should remain on the leg that braces against the axe.

A variation of this technique is to use the rope in the manner illustrated in Photo 45a. Here the loaded rope is passed underneath the boot and then around the ankle to create friction. To

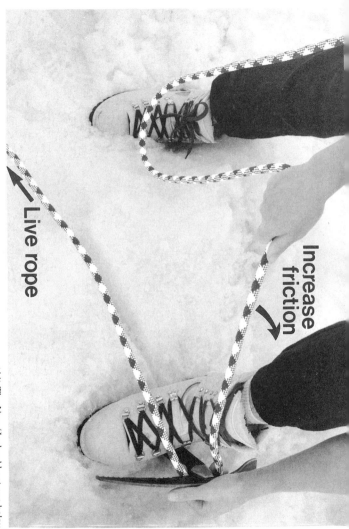

Live rope

Increase
friction

(44) The New Zealand boot axe belay

Live rope

(45a) The boot belay. Keep all your weight on the loaded foot.
Increase the friction by wrapping the rope around the ankle.

(45b) The boot belay. An ice axe is added for extra security

begin with you have to make a small platform for your foot and cut a small slot for the rope to pass through. The platform can be stomped out but the slot needs to be cut. In soft snow stomp down until you have a firm platform. Make sure that you keep some weight on the leg that has the rope wrapped around it as this will help to hold your foot in place whilst you are safeguarding someone. It is usually sufficient to use just the foot but an ice axe can be inserted if you need extra security (Photo 45b). On the whole this is a safer and more effective variation of the New Zealand foot brake.

A third method, popularly called the 'stomper belay', is effective in a surprising number of instances but will be found most useful for safeguarding a partner on easy-angled terrain; when probing for crevasses for example. The ice axe is driven vertically into the snow and a karabiner is clipped through the hole in the head. The rope to your partner passes through this krab and is safeguarded using a shoulder belay whilst standing on the head of the axe. Make sure that you stand well braced to take a load as it would be catastrophic if the rope were to slip off your shoulder (Photo 46). If you want to use this method on steeper slopes, the shoulder belay makes it quite unstable. Instead, you could belay the rope off your harness using a belay plate or Italian hitch.

It is a popular myth that some of the techniques described here can be employed to save a falling partner in an emergency when moving together. The New Zealand foot brake we are told, for instance, is used most effectively to stop someone by throwing all the coils away and driving the axe into the snow with the rope wrapped around it (as illustrated in Photo 44) and to gradually slow the falling climber by increasing the friction on the belay. Not only is this dangerous, it is also impossible to achieve except in situations where it is deliberately set up as a demonstration. Apart from anything else, by discarding the coils you are giving your falling partner more rope with which to gather momentum which immediately decreases the chances of

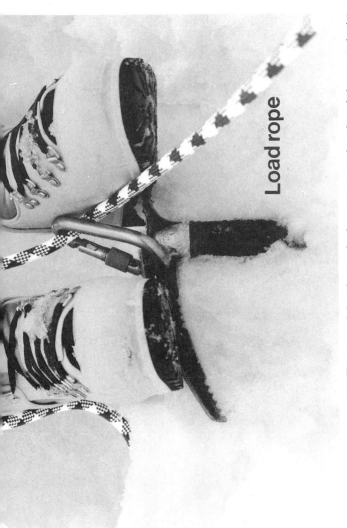

Load rope

(46) The stomper belay (the snow has been cut away to show the technique more clearly)

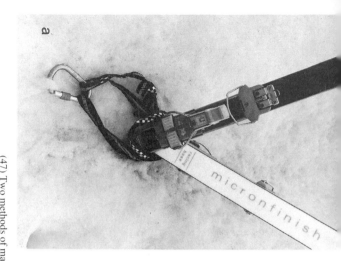

(47) Two methods of making an anchor from skis. They can also be buried horizontally. Try to place some padding around the ski edges before putting on the sling

holding the fall. The safest way and the best chance of holding a falling climber is to move on a short rope with few coils and be ready to correct a slip before it becomes a fall. On ridges the old saying 'if you fall into France I'll jump into Italy' is the most effective way to stop a fall. It does require quick reactions and plenty of 'bottle' however. See Moving Together page 184.

## Skis

Though it may seem somewhat out of place to discuss ski anchors here, many of the the rope techniques described in this book are applicable to ski touring.

There are three main types of ski anchors. Photos 47a and b shows two of the types. Note that in both methods the skis are tilted back slightly from the vertical. This makes them mechanically more sound and able to take a load more efficiently. In the example where the skis are parallel, the soles face outwards towards the load and in the crossed ski anchor the soles face each other. In both cases you should make an attempt to put some kind of padding over the sharp edges of the skis. In snow of a poor, unconsolidated nature or very soft snow, the skis can be buried horizontally in much the same way as other buried items. The attachment sling goes around the centre of the bindings and the skis are buried together sole to sole.

## ICE ANCHORS

The most reliable type of anchor to use in good ice is the ice screw. They come in a variety of shapes and sizes. There are basically two types. The drive-in screw-out and the screw-in screw-out.

The drive-in screw-out variety are quicker to arrange than the second type and for this reason are more convenient to place as running belays. However, they have a tendency to shatter hard or brittle ice and cause what's known as 'dinner plating' – a disconcerting occurrence where the ice breaks away in big

(48) Placing an ice screw. Start off with a small hole made with the pick then hammer gently and turn at the same time (a). Once the screw begins to bite, use the pick of an axe or hammer or a second screw to increase the leverage (b). Make sure it goes in to the hilt

chunks around the screw. The drive-in screw-out tubular variety are much less likely to cause this as they displace the ice up the tube.

Screw-in screw-out ice screws are a little slower to place and often require both hands to place properly. It is necessary to make a small hole to start the screw off. They are placed by turning and tapping at the same time until you feel it bite. Once it has bitten you can then use the pick of the ice axe or another screw to continue turning (Photos 48a and b). There are some makes of screw-in screw-out that are possible to fix in by turning with the hand nearly all the way. These types are distinguishable by the three or four cutting teeth at the end. Titanium screws are particularly easy to place by hand.

You must remember to clear the ice out of all tubular screws as soon as you take them out, for if the temperature is below freezing the ice will stay locked inside the tube and you won't be able to use the screw until it has melted out.

Whenever you anchor with ice screws you must try to use at least two and make sure that they are placed at least 45 cm (18 in) apart (Photo 49a) so that one screw does not weaken the ice around another. If, when you are placing a screw, it reaches a point where it will not go in any further, the chances are that you will have hit rock. Don't try to force it because you may push the ice off the face or bend the screw. Any ice screw that cannot be inserted right up to the eye should be tied off with a clove hitch on the screw right up against the ice (Photo 49b).

Sometimes in hot or sunny weather, particularly when practising techniques on a glacier, ice screws conduct heat and can melt out. Try to cover them over with ice or some other suitable item of kit and this will slow the process down.

### Ice Bollard

The same principles apply here as they do to the snow bollard, though of course an ice bollard does not have to be quite so large as a snow bollard. They are quite time-consuming to cut so it is

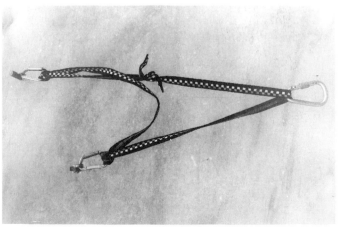

(49a) Two ice screws as an anchor *left*. See also Photos 55b and c for other methods of bringing two anchors to one central point
(b) A tied off ice screw *above*. The sling is clove hitched around the screw and placed as close to the ice as possible to one central point

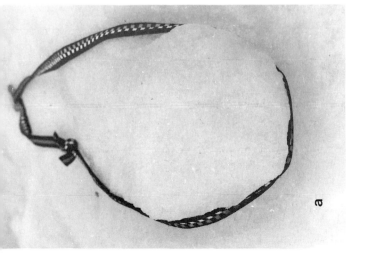

(50) An ice bollard (a) and an ice thread (b)

always better to try to look for a suitable feature to fashion one out of. This will cut the work down considerably. As they don't have to be quite so large it is sometimes possible to anchor to them via a sling around the bollard. You must ensure that there is a good lip at the back to hook the rope or sling under (Photo 50a).

## Ice Thread

An effective ice thread can be achieved by making two holes in the ice with an ice screw. The holes should begin at least 25 cm (10 in) apart and meet deep in the ice. The problem is of course to get the holes to meet. A sling, preferably a piece of rope because it's easier to thread, is then threaded through and the ends tied with either a double fisherman's or a ring bend. Photo 50b shows the finished product to prove that it can be done!

It is also possible to thread icicles, but only use really thick ones and even then be wary of their strength. Always put the sling around the lower part of the icicle. If using them as an anchor from which to belay you should always back them up with an ice screw or any other anchor.

## Ice Tools

You can anchor yourself to an ice tool or both tools placed in the ice. You must make sure that the placements are as good as you can possibly achieve and also that the wrist loops are in a good, strong condition. When using two tools, try to bring both wrist loops to one central point and clip the two together with a single karabiner. Try to back them up with a second type of anchor, such as an ice screw for extra security.

## METHODS OF TYING IN TO ANCHORS

Having described a wide variety of methods of creating anchors on the mountain, this next section looks at the options available for securing yourself in order to belay a companion.

The methods can be split in to the following categories:
1.    The rope directly around the anchor or anchors
2.    The rope attached to the anchor or anchors with a karabiner
3.    The rope into multiple anchors brought to one central point
4.    The anchor directly into the harness

We will consider each separately. Remember all the time that without exception you should always be fixed tightly to your anchor and be standing or sitting in a position that anticipates the direction of loading.

If you allow slack in the tie off to the anchor you will be jerked forward until your weight comes on to the anchor and if you are off to one side of the anticipated direction of loading, you will be pulled into line if someone falls off. A combination of the two basic errors is often disastrous. Think carefully – it is an important aspect of the safety chain.

## 1. The Rope Direct

The rope can be looped directly over a block or spike of rock and the end secured to the harness with a figure of eight knot tied through the central loop (Photo 51a). The rope could be secured equally well using a clove hitch into a karabiner or a figure of eight knot tied into a bight of rope and clipped via a karabiner into the central loop or tie on point. If you have more than one anchor point to tie into you must take the slack rope and repeat the process.

Using the rope to tie directly into anchors does take up a fair length of the rope and so is not commonly done. It is most useful in situations where you have run out of gear or the block or flake you want to tie around is too large for a sling.

If you are tied on with the rope directly around your waist you tie off from the anchor into the rope that goes around your waist.

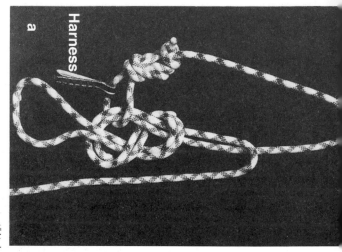

(51) A figure of eight tied back from the anchor to the central loop (a) and a figure of eight tied directly in to the anchor (b)

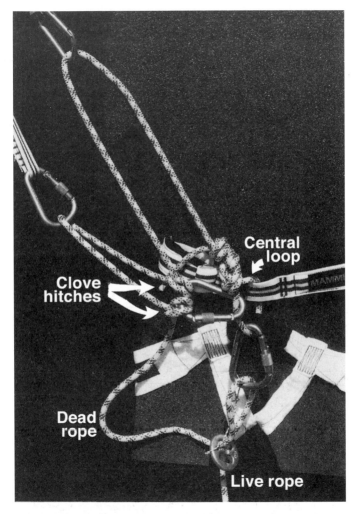

(52) Tying in to anchors – with clove hitches back to the central loop

## 2. The Rope through Karabiners on the Anchors

There is very little difference between this and the previous heading. However, there are one or two subtle differences that make it much easier and more versatile.

The simplest way to secure yourself to the anchor is with a figure of eight knot tied in a bight of the rope and clipped in to a screwgate karabiner on the anchor (Photo 51b). You could equally as well use a clove hitch directly into the krab. The drawback with this method is that if you have to stand out of arm's reach of your anchor, it can be difficult to gauge the correct length of the attachment in order to get tight to the anchor. My recommendation, therefore, is to only attach yourself in this way if you are within arm's reach of your anchor point. You will also find it inconvenient to attach to multiple anchors.

If you do have to move out of arm's reach of your anchor or anchor points, the system illustrated in Photo 52 will be found significantly more convenient. Take the main climbing rope and clip it into the first of the anchor krabs. Don't tie a knot, just pass it through the krab. Screw up the gate. Take the rope back to a large pear-shaped krab which is attached to the central loop and secure it with a clove hitch or figure of eight. The clove hitch is more easily adjustable. To tie into the second anchor point simply repeat the same process. You could go on *ad infinitum* like this but obviously there comes a point where it would be overkill.

If both anchors are a long way from the stance, take the rope and clip it in to the first anchor. Then run it through the krab on the central loop, from there take it through the second anchor point krab. You now have a sort of 'M' shape of ropes which act like a pulley system. Use the friction generated to lower yourself back down to the stance whereupon you secure the rope that runs through the central loop krab and the rope that ultimately goes to your partner. It may of course happen that the second anchor point is within arm's reach. In this case you can tie into it directly with a clove hitch or figure of eight (Photo 53).

(53) Tying in to anchors – the main one is clove hitched to
the central loop and the second direct to the anchor

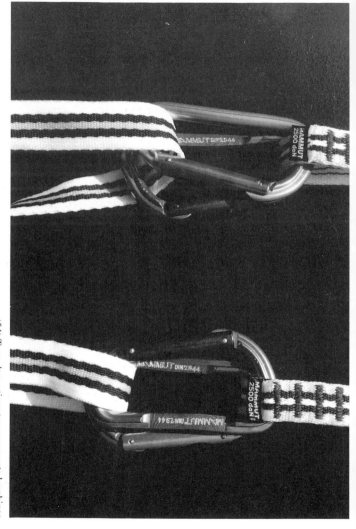

(54) Two alternatives to a screwgate karabiner

A word or two here about the use of screwgate karabiners on anchors. Whenever you attach a rope to your harness or central loop I recommend that you use a screwgate karabiner. I also recommend that you use one for your main anchor attachment. Any secondary anchors could be connected with a snaplink provided that you assure yourself that it is safe to do so. Climbers tend not to carry enormous numbers of screwgate krabs so if you do find yourself requiring the reassurance of a screwgate, and you don't have one to hand, rig up two snaplinks back to back or gates opposite as illustrated in Photo 54.

### 3. Multiple Anchors to One Central Point

Occasionally it may be convenient to bring two or more anchors to one central point of attachment. This can be done in a number of ways. One thing that you must remember though whenever you connect into multiple anchors is that if one anchor were to fail the load must come on to the secondary ones without any shock loading. Two anchor points can be brought together into one point if it so happens that the slings are of equal length. If they are not equal it may be possible to shorten them by tying a knot in the longest or extending the shortest.

There are three methods of using a single sling to bring anchors to a central point:

Photo 55a shows clove hitches tied at the anchor krab and the attachment point. The shock loading should one anchor fail will be negligible. It is possible to use this without the clove hitch at the central attachment point but you need to be certain that both the anchors are equally sound. This gives the advantage of being able to change your position on the stance yet maintain an equal loading on both anchors.

Photo 55b shows two anchor points brought together with a sling tied at the central attachment point with an overhand knot. If you don't tie an overhand knot and simply clip in to the doubled sling between the two anchors, you have a very dangerous and incorrect way of tying into two anchors, yet one that is com-

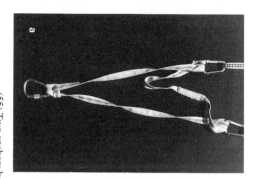

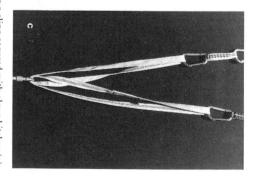

(55) Two anchors brought to a central point of attachment: using a sling secured with clove hitches (a); a sling tied with an overhand knot (b); and a sling with a twist in it (c)

monly seen. It will be immediately obvious that should one anchor fail the whole system will come undone. One often sees bolts connected in this manner, particularly on pre-rigged climbs or abseil descents. You should always rearrange the anchor more safely. What price for a life?

Photo 55c shows two anchor points brought to a central point with a twist in the sling. This is quick to rig but if one anchor fails you cannot avoid a shock loading on the other. Be sure that both anchors are equally sound.

## 4. Clipping in Directly to the Anchor

There is very little to be said about this method except that it is obviously very convenient should the occasion arise. You must of course be sure that the attachment is the correct length. I would also not recommend you to be too close to the anchor. For instance it would not really be practical to clip yourself in directly to a wire runner or the eye of a peg or ice screw. Let common sense prevail!

# Abseiling

## FIGURE OF EIGHT DESCENDEUR

Many people carry a figure of eight descendeur with them on all climbs. It is not a vital piece of kit by any means because many alternatives do exist. My feeling is that unless an item of kit has more than one function then it is probably not worth carrying. While it is true that the figure of eight can be used both for abseiling and belaying, its level of performance in the latter is a little limited. However, if you know that you have to do a lot of abseiling on your day out it may be worth taking one along.

A problem that sometimes occurs when doing multiple abseils is that the descendeur becomes too hot too handle. I'm sure that many climbers have been caught unawares a few times on hot sunny days. There's nothing that brings one back to reality quite like a scalding hot figure of eight dropping on to bare legs after pulling the rope through at the end of an abseil! Although it does become very hot there should be no danger of it melting the rope. It is generally accepted that the bulk of aluminium should dissipate the heat more efficiently than other abseiling devices.

Essentially the figure of eight is a fairly foolproof device for abseiling. There is however one point that is worthy of consideration (Photo 56). If you set up the device as shown in (a) it may happen that while you are negotiating a lip of an overhang or roof the descendeur becomes trapped against the lip and the rope flicks up over the device and the whole thing jams up (b). If this happens and you are unable to take the weight off the rope because you are hanging free, you may have a major epic on your hands. To avoid this situation occurring set it up as shown in (c). There are some devices available that have horns on the large ring which serve to prevent the larksfooting problem and so you don't have to be quite so careful in rigging them up.

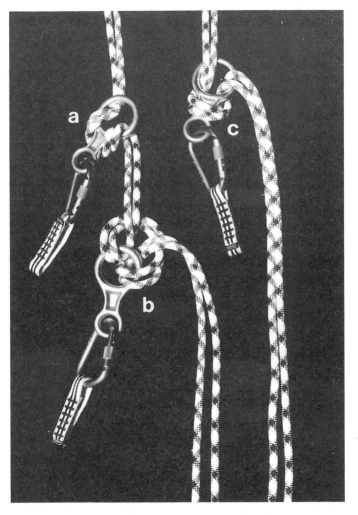

(56) The figure of eight descendeur

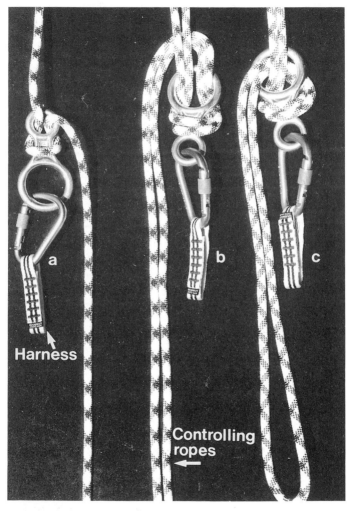

(57) (b) and (c) show a way of locking off the figure of eight

It is also possible to use the small hole of the figure of eight in the same way as the large one. Once again be particularly careful to ensure that the rope can't flick over the top (Photo 57a). This is a particularly useful method if you are abseiling on a single 9 mm (⅜ in) rope.

Though unlikely with a figure of eight, you may find that there is not enough friction to control the speed of descent. Should this be the case simply take the controlling rope under your thigh and control the speed of descent by wrapping the rope around your leg (Photo 58a). This method works for other 'mechanical' methods of abseiling too.

The most effective way to lock off a figure of eight, or indeed any other form of mechanical abseil device, is by re-peated turns of the controlling rope around the thigh or one turn around your waist. The turn around the waist is perhaps a little more efficient and safe. Turns around the thigh tend to fall down and may come completely undone. This cannot happen with the turn around the waist. Furthermore it is possible to leave the rope around your waist and feed it out gradually if you want to descend a little at a time. This will be found particularly useful in self-rescue situations (Photo 58b). Both these methods apply to most 'mechanical' methods of abseiling. A third way to lock off the figure of eight is illustrated in Photos 57b and c. This is very secure but sometimes difficult to arrange if you are unable to get just a little bit of weight off the rope.

## THE BELAY PLATE

Belay plates can also be used for abseiling. Unfortunately they have a tendency to twist the ropes quite badly and can jam up at inconvenient times. Of greater significance, though, is the fact that some ropes will slide through the plate more smoothly than others. This problem can also occur if abseiling on ropes of different thicknesses. This presents a serious problem if you are abseiling on double ropes threaded around an anchor in order to

(58) Increasing the friction on descent: two more turns around the thigh will lock it off (a). A way of increasing the friction that will also lock if you let go of the controlling rope (b)

recover them afterwards. If one rope does not run as smoothly as the other it creates a certain amount of creep around the anchor and may cause the ends to become unequal in length. As you might imagine, if this occurs high on a cliff during the descent it could present a very serious situation. For 'smoother' abseiling you should connect the plate to the harness with double krabs.

A general point about abseiling worth making here is that there is always noticeably more effective friction at the start of an abseil than there is further down. On a long steep abseil you may find it difficult to get moving at first and have to actually push the rope through the device. Nearer the end of the descent it may be all that you can do to hang on to the rope. Though not always practical you should consider using leather gloves for abseiling.

## THE ITALIAN HITCH

This is a suitable method of abseiling but subject to the limitations discussed on page 22.

## KARABINER BRAKES

Probably the most versatile abseil device. Setting up a karabiner brake requires no more equipment than the climber would normally carry. Though it is preferable and safer to set up with screwgate krabs it can also be set up using snaplinks. With practice it is possible to set the brake up to generate as much or as little friction as is required.

There are a number of different ways to set up a krab brake. Whichever set-up you use it is important to ensure that under no circumstances will the rope rub on the gate of a krab and cause it to open accidentally. Photo 59 shows a straightforward way to set up the brake and also a simple yet very effective way of increasing the friction and ultimately the control. It is very easy to overkill on the friction to such an extent that you may be

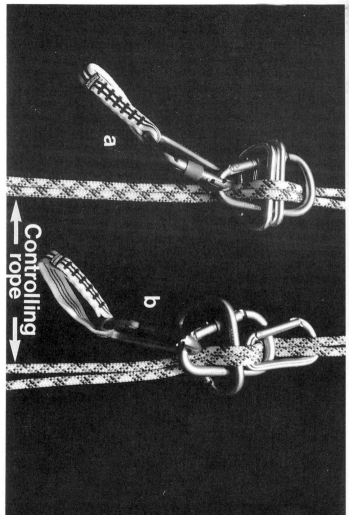

Controlling rope

(59) The karabiner brake: a simple two bar brake (a) and a way of creating slightly more friction (b)

unable to move! This is particularly the case if using double 11 mm (⁷⁄₁₆ in) ropes. In 'normal' circumstances the number of krabs used in the set-up illustrated is sufficient. The only time one may need more friction is after Christmas lunch or when lowering two people such as in improvised rescue.

It is really only worth using karabiner brakes with double rope. It requires a great many krabs to set up enough friction with a single rope. A word of warning – the krab brake is quite complicated to set up and can be set up dangerously, so be sure you practise it well before putting it to the test in a real situation. You would be well advised to use similar krabs throughout the brake as this makes operation much smoother. Make sure that the krab that supports the bar krabs is fairly large. If it is much smaller than the bar krabs the brake can slip off if, for some reason, you take your weight off the rope. They don't become completely detached but will give you a nasty shock when you put your weight back on the abseil rope. There have been many climbers who have discovered the folly of pulling the rope through the brake at the end of the abseil only to find the brake bar krabs go tumbling away – fun on sea cliffs. It is worth considering that if you do use karabiner brakes each time you abseil, modern lightweight karabiners are prone to damage by dirty or gritty ropes. This can cause an excessive amount of wear on the krab, weakening it to no small degree.

## PITON BAR BRAKES

This simple but effective device can be set up using a karabiner and an angle piton. It is very quick to set up and it is possible to generate more friction by adding a karabiner in the same way as that used on a karabiner brake (Photo 60). Be careful to ensure that the piton has no rough edges that may damage the rope. This method of abseiling would be most appropriate to winter or Alpine climbing where one would normally carry a few pitons.

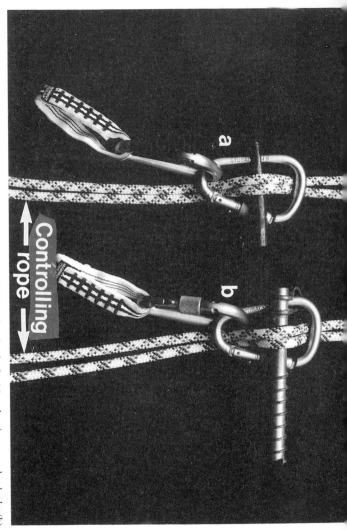

(60) Other brakes: piton bar brake (a) and an ice screw bar brake (b)

## THE ABSEIL RACK

A large and cumbersome device more appropriate to caving than climbing but nevertheless one that merits consideration in situations of Outdoor Centre 'production line' abseiling. It is less destructive to ropes and one can generate as much or as little friction as required by adjusting the distance between the bars and the number of bars used.

## 'CLASSIC' METHODS OF ABSEILING

There are a number of methods of 'classic' abseiling, all of which require the rope to be wrapped around some part of the body in order to create enough friction to control the speed of descent. My feeling is that all of these methods should only be used in emergencies – situations where no technical equipment other than a rope is available.

The proper classic abseil is rigged by standing astride the ropes facing the anchor point. Reach down with your right hand and bring the rope up behind your right thigh, across your chest, over your left shoulder and back into your right hand. The friction is controlled by bringing the right hand round your front for more friction and away from you for less.

Another form of classic abseil is to make up a Dulfer seat harness and take the abseil rope up through the karabiner, over the left shoulder and across the back into the right hand. This generates little friction and is also dangerous as clothing can get trapped in the karabiner.

*Note*: if you are left-handed please read left for right and right for left.

You should not really use any of these methods of abseiling on a single rope and neither can you use the safety back-up method of holding the end of the rope to stop someone in difficulty (see Abseil Safety below).

When using the 'proper' classic abseil you will find it more comfortable to twist sideways and lead with the right foot (left for left-handers). This is particularly important when stepping down over obstacles as leading with the other foot may cause the rope to ride up around the knee, causing you to flip upside down.

## ABSEIL SAFETY

Sadly, there have been some tragic abseiling accidents over the years. Some may reasonably be attributed to fate while others to errors of judgement. Truth to tell, abseiling is a very simple and straightforward exercise but it is this simplicity that leads to a complacent attitude and accidents.

Always check the abseil anchor thoroughly. Don't trust old decayed slings or in situ pegs or nuts if you are the slightest bit suspicious of them. It is cheaper to sacrifice a bit of gear rather than a life.

Simple safety precautions like tying a knot in the end of the ropes if you know or aren't sure that they reach the ground. It is also possible to rig a very simple 'safety back-up' system while abseiling. This is best effected by putting a French prusik (page 48) on the ropes above the abseil device. The prusik is then attached to the harness with a sling. As you abseil you simply keep one hand on the rope above the French prusik and slide it down with you. If you let go of it for whatever reason it should jam and halt further descent. It is vitally important to ensure that when the load is applied to the prusik that it does not stretch out of arm's reach. If it does then you will find it very difficult to release it again. The best gauge for the length of the attachment is for the prusik to be a slightly bent arm's length away from you when the sling comes tight. I would not recommend the use of any other prusik knot for this purpose. Many of them would jam solid and the only way to release it would be to cut it with a knife. The French prusik is the only one that can still be relied upon to be released even under load.

Another form of abseil safety is to hold the the bottom of the abseil ropes whilst someone is descending. If the abseiler loses control during the descent the person at the bottom should pull the rope very hard. This will halt any further descent until the tension is released. I have seen this used to great effect on a number of occasions which would have otherwise resulted in serious injury. Please note that 'classic' methods of abseiling do not respond to this method of safety. Indeed it would be down-right dangerous to even contemplate this.

If you are the first person down the abseil and you have perhaps had to pendule or move slightly to the side of the natural hang of the ropes, it may be worth considering fixing the ropes to the anchor for safety and to make life easier for the next person to descend.

To facilitate the separation and recovery of abseil ropes it is often worthwhile to clip a short sling and krab on to one of the ropes and the other end of the sling to your harness. If you do this at the beginning of the descent it will keep the ropes separated all the way to the bottom. Furthermore if you put it on the rope that you have to pull to retrieve the abseil ropes, it serves as a reminder of the correct rope to pull. It is becoming quite common practice to use a figure of eight knot for joining two ropes together for abseiling. Through long habit the thought is slightly off-putting but there is a tremendous advantage. If you join the two ropes in this way when you come to retrieve the ropes after the abseil the knot presents a flat profile to the edge that it may be dragged over. There is therefore much less chance that the knot could jam during retrieval.

If you are unfortunate enough to get your ropes jammed, be particularly careful how you go about freeing them. Don't ever for instance, attempt to climb up a single jammed rope if it is avoidable. It may not be as jammed as it first appears.

## ABSEILING PAST A KNOT

There are really very few occasions when it is necessary to join ropes together to add to the length it is possible to abseil. However, for the odd occasion where it may be necessary to abseil past a knot it is certainly a useful thing to know about.

It is possible to abseil straight over a knot in a single 9 mm (⅜ in) rope, if you are using a figure of eight descendeur. If you are hanging free it can be difficult to feed the knot through the device but this problem can be overcome to a certain extent by having long 'tails' on the joining knot which lead the knot into the device more evenly. I would venture to suggest that you only abseil on single 9 mm (⅜ in) rope as a last resort because there is very little friction and it can be difficult to hold such a thin rope.

If using a karabiner brake or a belay plate the situation is very different as the knot won't pass through the device. If there is a convenient ledge which coincides with the knot then simply abseil to the ledge, put in some protection for yourself whilst you take the rope out of the device and reconnect it below the knot.

Abseiling past a knot while hanging free or with no convenient ledge to stand on presents different problems. These are by no means complicated or insurmountable but will require practice in a safe and controlled situation.

If you know that you have to abseil past a knot before you set off, rig a safety back up French prusik as previously described. It is important to connect the French prusik to the harness with its own screwgate karabiner and in such a way that the abseil device can easily be removed whilst hanging from the French prusik.

Abseil down until the joining knot is 25–30 cm (10–12 in) away from the device (Photo 61a). This much coincide with your full weight coming on to the French prusik. Take the abseil rope out of the device and put it back on below the knot (Photo 61b), then make sure that the joining knot sits up against the device. Lock off the device securely: reach up and put one hand on the rope above the French prusik. By pulling down smoothly but firmly on top of the prusik it will release

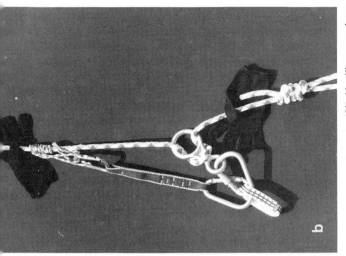

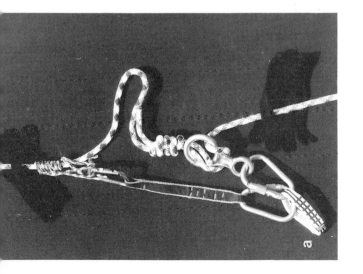

(61) Abseiling past a knot

and your weight will come back on to the abseil device. Once your weight is back on the device disconnect and release the French prusik. Unless you have a second knot to pass, it is probably not worth putting it back on, though you may want it for a safety back-up. Using this system it is possible to abseil past a knot in less than 30 seconds, not the usual 30 minutes as is often seen!

Please note that proper preparation is vital to smoothness and safety. The length of the French prusik and the distance you stop above the know are both crucial. On no account should you let the prusik go out of arm's reach and neither should you allow the knot to come closer than 25 cm (10 in) before your full weight is taken on the prusik. This system can also be used if you are lowering someone on two ropes joined together and need to pass the knot through the lowering device. The same principles of safety and technique apply, though it would be true to say that the length of the French prusik is not quite so critical (see page 73) – provided it is not too short!

# Ascending a Fixed Rope

There are few occasions in normal day to day climbing that require the ability to ascend a fixed rope. Situations where you might have to do so include emergency situations such as during the rescue of an injured climber or escaping from a crevasse; on a 'Big Wall' route where the second often climbs the rope for speed or for seconding artificial climbs. A mechanical ascending device is also used as a method of safeguarding yourself on long mountaineering routes where fixed ropes are left in place to assist with rapid ascent and descent of the mountain. Though in that situation the rope rarely bears the full weight of the climber.

The techniques can be broadly categorized into methods that employ a mechanical device, such as a Jumar and those that rely on loops of cord, such as the prusik knot, wrapped around the rope. By coincidence the two techniques are popularly called 'Jumaring' (using any mechanical device) and 'Prusiking' (when using a knotted loop). The first category is by far the most efficient and the second although less so is the best that can be done in an emergency situation.

Whichever you choose to use the basic technique of ascent is the same. A long sling or loop is used for the foot and a shorter one attached to the harness. These two slings or loops are more than adequate and there is no need to resort to using three loops as people have done in years gone by. The sit harness loop is connected *above* the foot loop. It is possible to do it the other way around but the margins of safety are less and it is more awkward to work. The ideal length of each loop can only be determined by practice and is ultimately dependent on the size and agility of the individual.

As a rough guide to the length of the sit harness loop, put a prusik knot on the rope and attach it to the harness via a karabiner. The prusik knot itself should be at about forehead-level when you are hanging in your harness and the loop is tight. The length of the foot loop is best determined by hanging from the sit loop with a prusik knot on the rope. Put your foot in the bottom of the loop and bend your leg to the point where you feel you could most comfortably stand up from (Photo 62). The efficiency with which you prusik is measured by the amount of height you gain when you stand up straight in the foot loop each time. If you can bend your leg behind your ear and still stand up on it then you will probably have reached the maximum efficiency. The same principles apply to determining the length of sling for a mechanical device.

Movement up the rope is effected by standing straight legged in the foot loop and moving the sit loop up. It is an energetic and quite tiring process to ascend a rope in such a manner, so be prepared to huff and puff a bit. It is very important to try to conserve energy, particularly if you have a long way to go. When you try to stand in the foot loop, make sure that you do so by pushing with your leg directly underneath you. Have the rope running up your chest all the time. Try to avoid hanging out backwards and having to pull yourself up with your arms. You will also find it easier if your foot loop is larksfooted around your foot to prevent it slipping out. If one leg gets tired of doing all the work simply swap feet or even use both feet in the loop.

If you have a chest harness on it is worth considering clipping the rope through a karabiner attached to the chest harness. This helps to keep you close in to the rope. You can also clip in the foot loop to the harness though unless you are using a system where the foot loop is fixed above the sit loop, this can be more trouble than it is worth.

For reasons of safety it is advisable that you consider tying a figure of eight knot at 5 m (15 ft) intervals as an extra back up. This knot can then be clipped into the central loop of your harness so that if for some reason the prusiks or devices should fail you do at least have something to stop you falling off the rope.

If you have a large or heavy rucksack on your back it is well worth taking it off and putting it on the rope below you. This acts as a weight to hold the ropes taut and actually makes it easier to move the loops or devices up the rope.

(62) Ascending a fixed rope: using prusik loops (a) and mechanical devices (b)

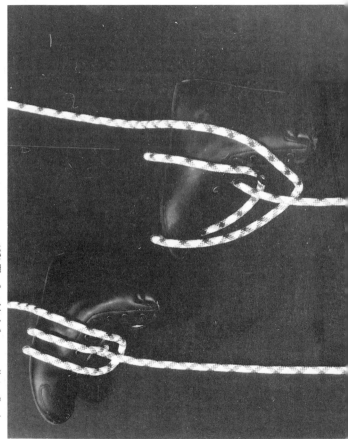

(63) The foot hitch for ascending a fixed rope

For relevant knots to use for prusiking refer to the section on 'prusik' knots (page 44).

## IMPROVISED ASCENT METHODS

If you find yourself with only one prusik loop it is quite possible to improvise in a number of ways and the following methods work well.

Put the prusik on the rope and attach it to your sit harness. Sit back in it and lift your foot to the point from where you can most comfortably stand up. Wrap the rope a few times around your foot, hold the slack and loaded ropes together and stand up. Still standing, move the sit loop up until it is tight, sit back and repeat the procedure. Photo 63 shows a foot hitch alternative to the wrap around the foot. Make sure that you tie a figure of eight in the rope every 2 m (6 ft) or so and clip it back into the harness as a safety back-up.

A second method which is less tiring but potentially quite dangerous is to use a belay plate and prusik. The belay plate is attached to the harness and the prusik used as a foot loop above the belay plate. Slide the foot loop up as high as possible and stand up. At the same time, pull the rope through the plate. When standing at your maximum height, lock off the plate and sit back in your harness. *Beware!* If you let go of the controlling rope of the belay plate you will head earthwards very quickly. With that in mind, tie off back to the harness with a figure of eight knot more frequently than the other methods described. You could use the Alpine clutch in place of the belay plate. This is very much safer because you can arrange it so that you are only able to pull the rope through as you stand up. If you let go of it , it should jam up. The only disadvantage with this is that if, for some reason, you need to go back down the rope, it isn't possible without having to rearrange the whole set up.

# Escaping from the System

This is the term used to describe the technique of releasing oneself from the belay system and end of rope whilst ensuring the security of the climber you are responsible for, usually with their full weight hanging on the rope.

The reasons for having to 'escape' are too numerous to mention them all but an example might be that you are belaying your partner when a large rock is dislodged by a party above and renders him or her unconscious. Another typical example would be on a glacier where a member of the party falls into a crevasse. Whatever the reason for having to escape and help your partner you must initially overcome the problem of having their full weight hanging from you and being tied in to the anchors.

In the first instance it is important to establish the need to escape while the person is hanging on the rope. It may be possible to lower the victim down to a ledge or even to the ground before you escape. If that be the case many of your problems are instantly solved. And don't isolate yourself in your predicament, there may be other people around who are more than willing to assist.

## THE BASIC PROCEDURE

Whether practising or doing it for real, make sure that you can see a way out of the situation the whole time – always think 'what will happen if…?' Work logically and safely, and try to keep things as simple, as tidy and as straightforward as possible.

The sequence of photographs shows how to escape from the system most efficiently in the easiest of all situations – one anchor point within arm's reach (Photos 64, 65 and 66).

Proceed as follows. Tie off the belay plate; put a French prusik on the load rope and clip it back into the anchor (extend it with slings if it is not long enough). Slide the prusik forward until it is under tension but make sure that it remains within arm's

(64) Escaping from the system – stage one

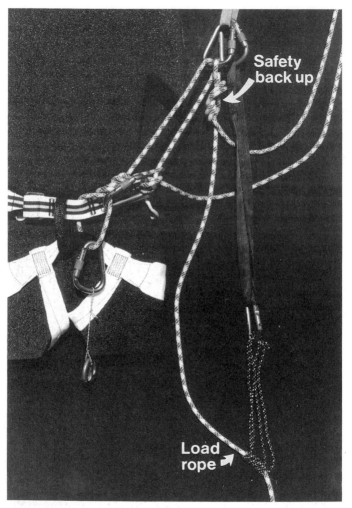

(65) Escaping from the system – stage two

(66) Escaping from the system – stage three

reach. Release the belay plate and gradually lower the weight on to the French prusik. All the weight should now be directly on the anchor point. Take the rope out of the belay plate and fix it back to the anchor with a figure of eight knot and separate krab (ensure that there is a little slack in the rope to allow for slippage and to facilitate unclipping later on). Untie yourself from the anchor making sure you clip into an alternative anchor for your own safety. Mind you don't drop your belay plate! Finally consider backing up your anchor as necessary.

It is worth noting that with some harnesses, mainly ones with a separate belt and leg loops, it is possible to escape by simply tying off the belay plate, undoing the harness and pulling it through the central loop. Some of these two-piece harnesses have little tabs through which the manufacturer recommends you to thread the rope when tying on. These tabs are purely to stop the rope sliding around in the harness but are not absolutely necessary and are certainly not load-bearing. If you do thread the rope through the tabs you will need to go through the longer process of escaping the system.

Having escaped, you are now free to move around at your leisure. You may have to descend to the person hanging on the other end of the rope, in which case use all the spare rope to abseil down on. If you are happy to abseil off the same anchor that your victim is hanging on then simply abseil off the rope on the other side of the figure of eight knot in Photo 66. If you are not happy to do this then you should rig another anchor for your abseil. For safety you should tie a knot in the end of the rope and use a French prusik safety back-up.

## DEALING WITH PROBLEMS

Inevitably problems will crop up. The most likely one to occur is that you are unable to reach the anchor point from your stance when doing the escape and before you can escape you must create a 'new anchor point'. To do this tie a prusik loop or a klemheist in a tape sling around both ropes going back to the anchor. Whichever knot you decide to use put in as many turns as you can. Do this as far back as you can comfortably reach (Photo 67) and clip in a karabiner. You now use this krab as your new anchor point and escape in the same way as described previously. It is very important that, once you have untied from the end of the rope, you tie knots that will prevent the new anchor from sliding off the end (Photo 68).

You may find yourself with two or even three anchors, each tied into separately with the rope. If it is possible, link all or a selection of the ropes together when tying the klemheist or prusik as described and use this as your new anchor. If this is not possible then you must put a klemheist or a prusik around each of the anchor ropes and link them together until they form one central anchor point. Remember that once you have escaped you will be in a position to back everything up as you see necessary.

It is of course terribly easy to get yourself into an awful tangle when escaping so you should practise in a controlled situation as much as possible before having to put it to the real test. It is a good idea to present yourself with situations to deal with on low-level practice crags – you can make them as simple or as ludicrously difficult as you like! For instance, if you are using a single rope and the victim is more than half the rope's length below you you will not have enough rope to reach him or her by abseil. In this case you must abseil down as far as you can and then transfer yourself on to the victim's rope and continue down by prusiking.

If you are climbing on double ropes or you have a spare rope, as you may do when travelling across a glacier, you would be advised to only tie off one rope when doing your escape. Although the other end may be tied into the victim, you will at least be able to use the full length as there will not be any tension in it. Once you get to the victim you can untie him or her from it completely thus giving yourself greater flexibility in coping with the situation.

Load rope

(67) Escaping the system when the anchor point is out of reach – stage one

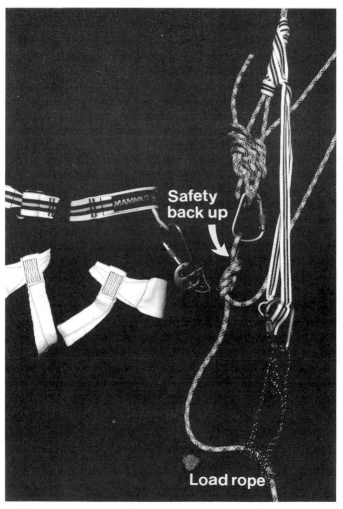

(68) Escaping the system when the anchor point is out of reach – stage two

There are almost certain to be running belays on the rope between you and the victim. You must decide what to do with them – leave them in or take them out – as you descend. So much depends on the situation that it is impossible to suggest a standard procedure. However, if by removing a running belay you are likely to cause the victim to move from their position, I would suggest that you leave it in.

## AFTER THE ESCAPE

Having escaped and gone down to your victim you may have to administer first aid and also rig him or her in some kind of full body harness for comfort. You must then decide what to do from this point onwards. What you do is obviously dependent on innumerable factors but your choice can be limited to four main courses of action:

1.  Return to the stance and lower the victim to the ground either in one go or in stages

2.  Return to the stance and hoist the victim to the same stance or to safety

3.  Leave the victim in situ while you go for help

4.  Evacuate yourself and the victim simultaneously (assisted evacuation)

### Lowering the Victim

Once you have decided to lower the victim we will assume that you have regained the stance and everything is set up and ready to go as in Photos 66 or 68. To convert the system to a lower, unclip the figure of eight and put the rope in an appropriate lowering device. Hold the controlling rope in one hand and with the other release the French prusik. The load should come on to lowering device as gradually as possible. Continue lowering with one hand keeping the French prusik, now an autobloc, released with the other. If you want to stop lowering and let go of the ropes for any reason the load should be taken by the autobloc. If you need to leave the system unattended for any length of time you should tie off the belay device in the appropriate manner.

If you can lower the victim to the ground in one go you are fortunate and should do so! To get yourself down you should tie off the lowering rope as soon as the victim reaches the ground. Have a little slack in the rope so that you can abseil down. It is really not worth messing around trying to retrieve rope and gear unless you need it to continue to civilization. You can always come back and collect it later – it might still be there! If you do not have enough rope to reach the ground in one lower then you must obviously do it in stages. This will be limited to a maximum of 22–25 m (70–80 ft) if you are climbing on a single rope and so can be very time consuming indeed.

The lower of each stage is fairly straightforward if you can trust your victim to rig a safe anchor for him or herself at the end of each lower. Proceed as follows. Lower the victim to a convenient stopping place or just under the halfway mark on the rope. Get them to rig an anchor and clip in securely. *They must not untie from the end of the rope.* Take the rope out of the lowering device and pass it through the abseil anchor and abseil on the double rope so that you can recover it once you reach the victim. Remember that at all times you must look to your own safety as well as that of the victim. On the abseil it is worth using a safety back-up.

Now let us consider what to do if you do not trust the victim or the victim is unable to rig a safe anchor at the end of each lower. Take the rope out of the the lowering device but leave the victim protected by the autobloc which remains attached to the anchor. Clip the rope through a krab on the anchor and throw the remaining slack, with a knot tied in the end, down the cliff. Put an abseiling device, preferably a belay plate, on the doubled rope for yourself and a safety back up. Untie the original autobloc which was left on to protect the victim and set off down. As you abseil the victim is protected by the fact that their rope passes around the abseil anchor, through your safety back-up and through the abseil device. The use of the belay plate makes this a safer device to use. In theory, if the victim were to roll off the ledge he or she should not fall too far. Once you reach the victim you should of course put in an anchor and before doing anything else clip yourselves into it. Retrieve your ropes and the procedure can be repeated all the way down the cliff or until you reach safety.

There are of course all sorts of variations to the techniques but having practised and mastered the basics you will soon learn what they are. Remember it is important to keep things as simple and as straightforward as possible.

## HOISTING

There are two basic types of hoist used in rescue situations: the assisted hoist and the unassisted hoist. Before undertaking a hoist in a rescue situation you should be absolutely certain that this is what you need to do. If your victim is a 'dead' weight on the end of the rope it is often impossible for one person to hoist efficiently.

### Assisted Hoist

This hoist is by far the simplest to rig up and the most effective in use. It is particularly useful in a situation where your second is unable to climb a section of the route or has fallen off to one side and cannot get back on again. It can however be difficult for the victim to assist if he or she is hanging in space. It can be rigged very quickly and does not even require you to escape from the system if you are using any belaying device other than a body belay.

Proceed as follows. Tie off the belay device. Put an autobloc on the load rope and clip it back into the central loop on your harness. Make this attachment quite short, certainly no more than 30 cm (1 ft) from the device as you do not want it to slide down the rope and out of arm's reach. The load should now be predominantly on the anchor. Take up some slack rope and throw a loop with a krab clipped in to it down to the victim. Tell the victim to clip the krab into the central loop of their harness. Make sure that the rope is not twisted. Untie the belay plate and lower the victim's weight on to the autobloc.

You are now ready to hoist. The victim should pull on the rope that travels towards him or her. This is easy to establish – neither the victim nor the rescuer pulls on the rope that is tied to the victim and has the autobloc on it (load rope) and of the remaining two one of them comes down to the victim and the other back up to the belayer (Photo 69). Both the rescuer and the victim pull simultaneously and if the victim can walk up the crag or the slope it can be a simple matter to hoist them up. Should either of you need to rest at any time simply lower the weight on to the autobloc and let go with all hands. This is an ideal way to get over the crux moves of the climb!

Once you have hoisted far enough you will need to get back into the belaying mode again. This is simple enough to achieve but just remember to safeguard the victim before you sort everything out. This can be done most effectively by tying off the belay device.

Problems can occur with the system, especially if your victim is more than a third of the rope's length below you as the system requires three lengths of rope between rescuer and victim. Its use is also limited to situations where you are able to get a loop to the victim in the first instance. Communication is very important particularly if the victim does not understand how the system works. You must be able to converse without fear of the instructions being misinterpreted.

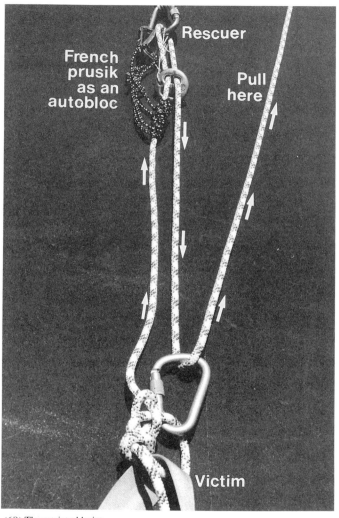

(69) The assisted hoist

## Unassisted Hoists

If you are unfortunate enough to find yourself in a situation where you have no option but to hoist your victim to a safe place then you are going to require patience, muscle power, plenty of space and lots of time. It would also be to your advantage to have a few pulleys around. This is possible in glacial travel but unlikely in a crag climbing situation. Do not underestimate the difficulties involved in hoisting someone without assistance. What is essentially a simple system to set up is extraordinarily difficult to effect.

There are a number of ways of hoisting. It might even be possible, if you're very strong and the victim light, to hoist by simply pulling your victim up hand over hand. If you do do this be sure to have some kind of safety back-up for when you need to rest or if you let go of the rope. A safer way of pulling someone up directly is shown in Photo 70. A prusik is attached to the load rope and then to the rescuer's harness, but keep it quite short. The load rope is then passed through an Italian hitch at the anchor and an autobloc to the load rope. The rescuer slides the prusik down the load rope as far as it will go and uses the powerful leg muscles to do the pulling while at the same time pulling the rope through the Italian hitch. To gain a rest the load is taken by the autobloc. This system is only effective if the rescuer has the strength to lift the victim but adaptations of the technique can be used in 'pulley' hoists, as will be seen later.

A brief word here about the mechanical advantage of the different systems. The hoisting systems we use in improvised rescue do not generally use pulleys at each turn of the rope so that a rope running over a single karabiner often creates so much friction that it negates the mechanical advantage gained. One rapidly approaches the point in attempting to increase mechanical advantage where there are so many 'pulleys' in the system that it is impossible to pull the rope through! By doubling up the karabiners at each turn you reduce the angle that the rope goes through and also the friction generated. Using lightweight

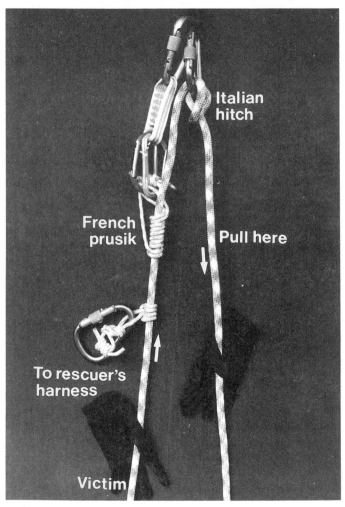

(70) The direct hoist

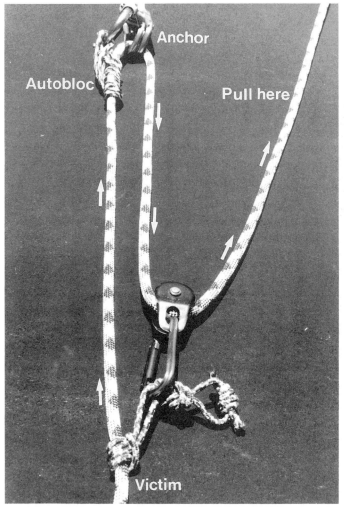

(71) The basic Z pulley

pulleys designed specifically for mountaineering reduces the friction generated and increases the effects of mechanical advantage. But it's another item of gear to carry.

An additional point worth mentioning is that in using climbing ropes much of the energy expended pulling someone up is used in taking the stretch out of the rope.

There are so many factors that go against hoisting that it is important to establish that it is really necessary before you begin.

## The Z Pulley System

The Z pulley system or the 'two in one hoist' as it is sometimes called is a good basic hoist to begin with and works well if there are plenty of helpers and plenty of room to manoeuvre.

Let us assume that you are on a stance and have decided to hoist. The set up is similar to that in Photo 66 or 68 having just escaped from the system. Take a spare prusik loop and put it on the load rope as far down as you can safely reach. Untie the figure of eight knot and pass it through a new karabiner or a pulley on the anchor, and then down through the prusik you have just put on (Photo 71). It is to your advantage to make this latter prusik connection as short as possible.

All the victim's weight should be hanging on the original French prusik which is now transformed into an autobloc. To hoist the victim you should pull on the rope that comes up from the prusik loop. Photo 71 shows direction of rope travel and where to pull. If the victim is able to 'walk' up the cliff then you should ask them to do so. You will probably find that it is only possible to move the victim a little at a time and so in between pulls rest by lowering the weight on to the autobloc. Eventually the prusik knot will come up to meet the autobloc. At this point take the load on the autobloc and slide the prusik back down as far as you can safely reach. Repeat the procedure until you are completely exhausted or the victim is where you want him or her to be.

If you have enough space then you can attach the pulling

rope to your harness with a belay plate or Italian hitch and use your leg muscles to pull rather than your arms. This is much less tiring. Pulling is effected by locking off the device and pulling in that position. Once you reach the limit of pull lower the victim on to the autobloc and move back down to the edge taking the slack rope in as you go.

*Improved Z Pulley*

To be truthful, the system previously described is very difficult to put into practice in a less than perfect situation, particularly when you have no other assistance. It is possible to improve the system slightly by a number of variants and I have found the following to be satisfactory.

Leave the system set up as before and on the pulling rope place a short prusik loop and karabiner. Tie the other end of the climbing rope into the anchor with a figure of eight knot. Bring some of the rope down to the new prusik and clip it through the krab (Photo 72a). You now have a new pulling rope and should find the whole set up much easier to pull yet you have only introduced one extra point of friction. If space is limited and it is easier for you to pull the rope downwards rather than up, rig up the new system so that the end of the rope clips in to the second prusik and you pull through the karabiner on the anchor (Photo 72b).

This system is much more efficient than the basic hoist, the only disadvantage being that you have to move the prusiks down the rope more frequently. However, the extra ease of pulling far outweighs this.

## The Yosemite Lift

This type of hoist was originally developed for sack hauling on the Big Walls of Yosemite in California, USA. It is still a widely used system for that purpose but has little to recommend it for hoisting people. It works most efficiently when the anchor points

(a)

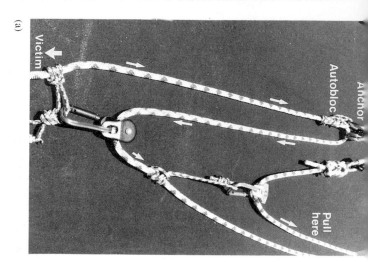

(b)

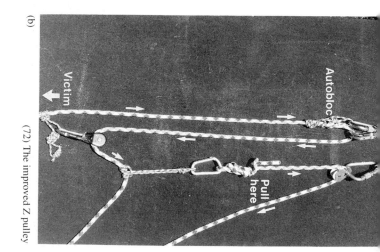

(72) The improved Z pulley

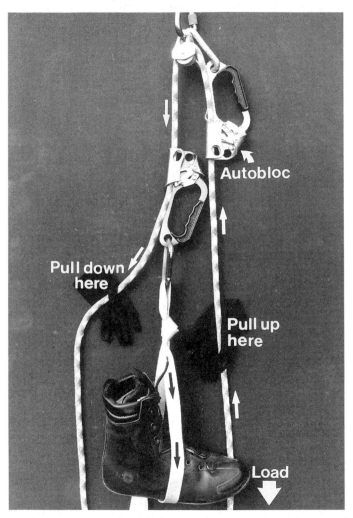

(73) The Yosemite lift

are above you.

When climbing multi-day climbs such as those found in Yosemite, it is quite likely that you will have mechanical ascending devices with you and these can be used in place of prusik loops to make life a little easier. Photo 73 shows the basic set up. It is well worth carrying the pulley for just this purpose if you go on a climb knowing that you will have to sack haul.

The autobloc is provided by a mechanical device placed upside down on the load rope. The load rope is then passed through a pulley in the anchor and a second mechanical device placed the right way up, with a short foot loop attached, on the pulling rope. As you push down on the pulling rope with your foot you should try to pull up the load rope with the other hand.

## ASSISTED EVACUATION

One day you may find yourself in a situation where you have no option but to evacuate both yourself and an injured victim who is unable to assist in any useful way. The 'traditional' way to do this has been to use an improvised rope Tragsitz. In truth, to the climber or mountaineer with limited resources it is not a feasible system of evacuation. There are a number of reasons for this, not least that it requires an extra rope, which is in itself an unlikely luxury. It is very difficult indeed to get someone on your back if you do not have anyone else to help you; it requires a good large ledge to work from each time; if any problems arise they are difficult to deal with; if the victim requires medical attention during the descent you have to stop, get him off your back, then back on... It is hardly a practical method.

The system I prefer to use is basically one in which both the rescuer and the victim abseil together from the same device, with the rescuer doing all the controlling. In this position the rescuer is allowed full flexibility and can carry the victim in the position that is most practical and comfortable. It is even possible to change positions as often as you wish on the way down. You can have the victim in front of you, by your side walking down with you, behind you, across your lap, between your legs or even below you. There are no hard and fast rules to apply to what position the victim should be in, and so much has to be left to the judgement of the rescuer. The following guidelines may be of some help in deciding as to which position is most suitable.

1.   Very steep cliff/unconscious victim – across the rescuer's lap or hanging below. If you choose to have the victim hanging below, you must be very careful to ensure that you don't cause any further injury with your feet (Photo 74).

2.   Slabby terrain/unconscious victim – between the rescuers legs with the victim's legs pointing out from the crag (Photo  75).

3.   Any terrain/walking victim – side by side (Photo 76).

Whichever of the possible positions you decide to use the method of rigging the system is essentially the same. There is only one important variable to consider and that is the length of the sling attachment for both the victim and the rescuer to the descending device. For example, if the victim is to be across the rescuer's lap the victim's attachment must be shorter than the rescuer's. If both are to descend side by side then they must obviously be of equal length. Photos 77a and b show the simplified set up for both of these positions.

It is possible to rig an adjustable length attachment for both rescuer and victim or for one of them only. This requires extra equipment in the form or a length of 5 mm ($\frac{3}{16}$ in) or 6 mm ($\frac{1}{4}$ in) cord for each attachment so may not be practical for most situations. A cowstail with a number of possible attachments is much more versatile.

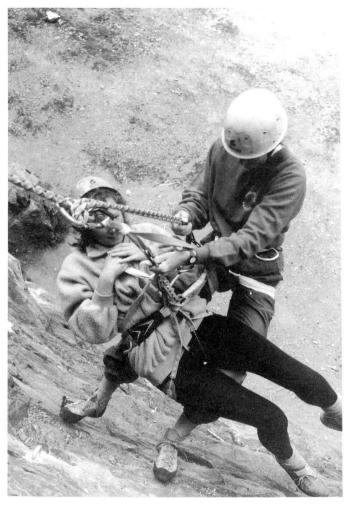

(74) Assisted evacuation: the victim across the rescuer's lap

(75) Assisted evacuation: the victim between the rescuer's legs

(76) Assisted evacuation: the victim and the rescuer side by side

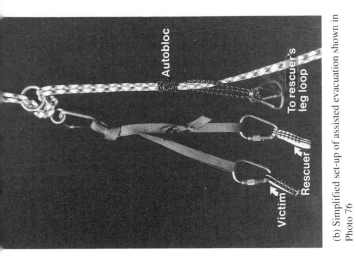

(b) Simplified set-up of assisted evacuation shown in Photo 76

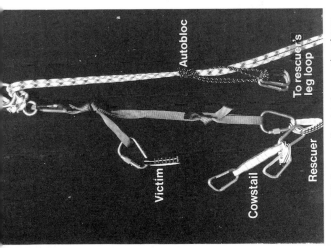

(77a) Simplified set-up of assisted evacuation shown in Photo 74

## THE DESCENT

The abseil device that you choose to use must generate sufficient friction to enable the rescuer to control the speed of descent of two people safely and effectively. A figure of eight abseil device or a belay plate is ideal. So also is a karabiner brake with extra friction bars. The Italian hitch generates enough friction but tends to twist the ropes and cause tangles, which is really the last thing you need to happen.

As with all these rescue situations, it is of vital importance to have some kind of fail safe system for extra security. The usual method of protecting an abseil, with the French prusik above the abseil device, is not suitable here because the device will almost certainly be beyond arm's length. Remember that the safety back up has to be well within reach. The alternative is to put the French prusik below the device and attach it to the rescuer's harness leg loop. Photo 75 shows this clearly. Lowering is then effected by the rescuer releasing the French prusik and allowing the rope to slide at the same time. If the rescuer lets go of the rope for any reason further descent will be halted as the French prusik comes tight. This method gives excellent fine control of the lower.

One minor disadvantage, and one that you need to be aware of, is that if the rescuer has let go with both hands to attend to something else, any movement upwards of the leg that has the French prusik attached will cause some rope to slide through the device. This is by no means a major problem but it is as well to be aware that it might happen.

You could attach the safety back-up French prusik to the front of the rescuer's harness. If you have the inclination it is worth trying in a practice situation but it is definitely not as effective as having it attached to your leg loop.

As you descend you will probably find it easier to have one hand on the victim's harness and the other on the controlling rope. If you need to pull the victim away from the crag, perhaps to lie across your lap or between your legs, use a cowstail to hold them in close to you. This should be clipped to the victim at the harness attachment point and to the rescuer anywhere on the harness that is convenient and comfortable. By pushing out from the cliff face with your legs you will find with relatively little effort it is possible to keep the victim away from the rock.

The ropes are rigged through the anchor in the same way as you would for a 'normal' abseil retreat from a climb and you descend on both ropes together. Thus, with single rope you are limited to 22–25 m (70–80 ft) abseils but with two ropes the full length of each rope. The ropes can be pulled down after each stage, making sure that you secure both you and your victim to the mountain first. Don't worry about leaving your gear behind – it is much more important to get you and your victim down without any problems occurring.

## An Alternative Method

The above system works very well and is versatile enough to cope with any situation you may find yourself in but it may be of interest to try out a slight variation. Instead of descending on doubled rope as above, clip the rope through the anchor karabiner, tie the victim into the end of the rope and attach yourself to the other side with a descending device. Photo 78 shows the basic set-up. You will see that in this method the anchor acts as a sort of pulley but the lowering is still done by the rescuer. It is important that both rescuer and victim are connected as imbalances in weight may cause one to move down the cliff faster than the other.

I have also seen this system operated using an abseil device at the anchor point but feel that if anything should go wrong with the device, such as it jamming up, when you are halfway down you will be in a terrible predicament. It is better to avoid it happening in the first place.

The only advantage with this alternative method over the

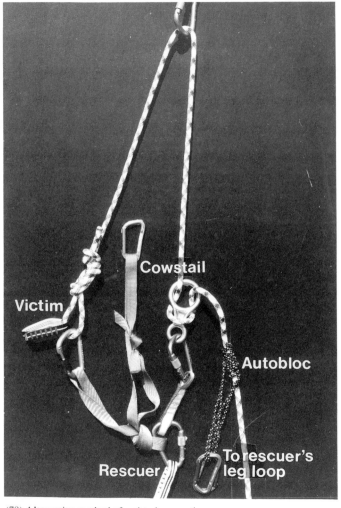

(78) Alternative method of assisted evacuation

standard one is that it is much easier and more immediate to adjust the positions of both the rescuer and the victim in relation to each other.

# Direct Belays and Belaying Techniques

In traditional climbing procedure climbers safeguard each other with some kind of body belay or mechanical device. In doing so the belayer is placing him or herself between their companion and the anchor point to which both are ultimately attached. This can simply be referred to as an *indirect* belay or one in which the initial impact of a fall is taken by the belayer. When using a *direct* belay the load comes immediately on to the anchor. In the case of an indirect belay, some of the strain can be taken by the belayer's body thereby decreasing the load on the anchor points. Indeed, in cases where the anchors are poor or a little suspect, this is done deliberately. In the case of a direct belay however, the load will come immediately on to the anchor. It may be stating the obvious, but your anchors must be 100% sound.

Direct belays should always be treated with the utmost caution and you should always question your decision to use one. There is no doubt whatsoever though that in certain situations a direct belay is both quick, convenient and efficient to use. These situations occur most commonly in moderate terrain where there may be some risk of a fall but not enough to warrant a full blown belay and stance. They occur in winter climbing quite frequently and the technique is in common usage in Alpine regions where, combined with moving together techniques (see page 184), it forms the basis of all Alpine ropework.

Direct belays can take on many guises. They may be rock spikes or flakes, large boulders, trees, chocks wedged in a crack, pitons, slings around chockstones, snow or ice anchors – in fact almost any kind of anchor commonly used in climbing.

The techniques of using each anchor vary too. You may drape the rope directly around a spike or you may place a sling around it instead and clip the rope in with an Italian hitch. Whatever the anchor and method you decide to use *always* remember that the set up must be able to cope with the full weight of a fall and that if it fails you are powerless to halt the consequences.

## USING THE ROPE DIRECTLY AROUND A ROCK OR TREE

After the soundness of the anchor the second most important consideration is to be sure that the rope will not slip off the anchor if you have to hold a fall. Sometimes the anchor may be quite shallow or rounded and not accommodate the rope effectively. The anchor, particularly if it is a spike or flake may also have sharp edges which abrade the rope and may even cause it to break when a load is applied. What is surprising to most people who use direct belays of this kind for the first time is the ease with which a fall, particularly that of a second, can be held. The amount of friction generated by a turn around even the smallest flake or spike can be impressive.

As a general rule in all direct belaying, the more rope you are able to have in contact with the anchor, the greater the friction will be. The greater the friction, the easier it is to hold a falling climber. It is important when belaying a second in this fashion that the rope is kept taut at all times and you should pay particular attention to the way in which the rope is taken in. Ensuring that you never let go of the controlling rope is crucial. To hold a fall more effectively grip the two ropes together with the hand that holds the live rope (Photo 79).

Unless you are able to arrange for a satisfactory upward pulling anchor, you should not use this particular method for belaying the leader. You can use direct belay techniques to belay a leader but only with upward pulling anchors and by connecting the rope to the anchor via a karabiner.

## USING THE ROPE THROUGH A KARABINER

If you decide that you are going to use a sling around a spike or

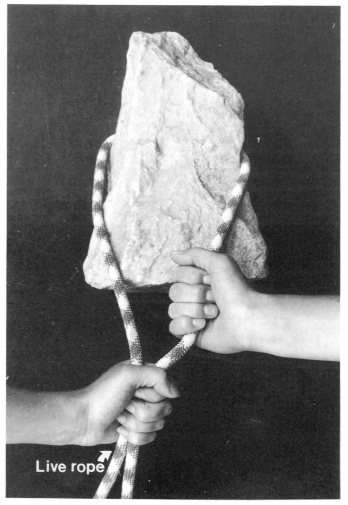

(79) Direct belay around a spike

a nut in a crack or a thread anchor, or bolts, pegs or ice screws you will have to connect the rope to the anchor via a karabiner.

You will have to use some sort of friction device in order to hold a fall. This could be a belay plate, a figure of eight descendeur or an Italian hitch. If you decide to use a belay plate make sure that you can operate it correctly by standing behind the plate (see page 71). In practice the plate is awkward to use and requires an almost purpose made stance to operate it safely so an Italian hitch or a figure of eight may be preferable. It is possible to operate both the latter devices from in front of the anchor, which will in fact be found more convenient in the majority of cases.

The rope can be used directly through the karabiner without any friction device at all. It is essential to wear leather gloves if you want to give yourself any chance of being able to hold someone. In unpractised hands however this is not a terribly safe method and if for some reason your partner falls off and you are unable to hold the rope, the consequences may well be fatal. You will no doubt see it used on the mountains however and that is the main reason for mentioning it here. The only term I've ever come across for this method is the 'Australian glove belay'. It is possible to make it a little safer by putting a second turn around the karabiner. This unfortunately has a tendency to twist the ropes quite badly.

A further consideration worthy of a few words is the combination of a belay device, such as a plate or hitch attached directly to the belayer or even a body belay, but with the rope running through or around a direct belay. This allows the belayer to hold the rope more easily yet utilizes the speed of a direct belay. In most cases it would not be necessary for the belayer to anchor to the mountain. Indeed if that was necessary it would negate the advantages of the direct belay.

# Moving Together

Moving together is the commonly used term for situations where two, or more, climbers are roped together for safety and moving up, down or across the mountain but do not go through the traditional sequence of making stances and climbing one at a time.

The technique is most often used in moderate terrain where there may be the potential of a serious slip or fall but in consideration of speed and efficiency of movement on the mountain it does not justify traditional belaying and climbing techniques. Such terrain includes easy but exposed scrambling, easy snow climbs and glacial travel. It is a tenuous form of safety that relies on good technique, quick reactions and an ability to handle ropes and equipment slickly.

It is a technique that is generally criticized in the UK for its apparent disregard of safety but one that is practised in Alpine regions more frequently than any other technique. In these pages I will try to dispel some of the myth but will make no attempt to denounce the serious implications of using it in the mountains.

## MOVING TOGETHER – TWO ON THE ROPE

This is moving together in its simplest form. Two climbers of fairly equal ability and experience and moderate rock scrambling terrain such as might be found on an easy classic Alpine peak or the Cuillin on Skye.

The first decision that has to be made is how much rope to have between the two climbers. This can be a problem because too much rope out may lead to complications and inevitably, tangles and not enough rope to greatly reduced safety margins. Unfortunately there is no hard and fast rule that can be applied as each situation dictates a different course of action.

A good starting point, however, is to have about 10 m (30–35 ft) between each climber. The remainder of the rope can be shared equally between the two people or carried by one person. If the decision is for one person to carry it, it is as well to give it to the more experienced as he or she will be the one most likely to need it. This will be particularly true if route-finding is a problem or having just surmounted a short section of difficult climbing, one finds that to go on a further 7 m (25 ft) or so will lead to a safer stance and/or better anchor.

Photos 80a and b and 81 show a recommended way to shorten the rope by coiling it around the body. There are many ways of tying the rope off at the harness but, though not usually dogmatic in my approach to these things, I suggest that this is one of the simplest and most effective. It is also particularly easy to release more rope as it is required.

When coiling the rope around your shoulder you should try to make each coil about waist length. Anything shorter will have you walking round like Quasimodo all day and anything longer will make you angry as you'll be tripping over the loops. Please remember that it is important to tie the coils off for safety reasons. If you don't and you have to hold a falling climber the coils will tighten up around your body and probably strangle you.

Most of the time you will find it easier to move with a few coils in your hand (Photo 82a). Here again make the coils quite short so that there is little risk of tripping over them. Make sure that you take coils working from the thumb outwards. This will allow you to drop coils easily as and when they are required. Photo 82b shows a good way to lock off the coils. If you have to change the coils to the other hand you must turn the whole bunch around before doing so. As a general rule you should always try to carry the coils in the downhill hand. This means that if someone falls off below you the rope is not pulled across your body as the strain comes on to it.

Photo 82c shows another method of carrying coils. This is called 'lapping' the rope and though favoured by some climbers it is certainly not as popular nor is it as easy to hold a 'falling'

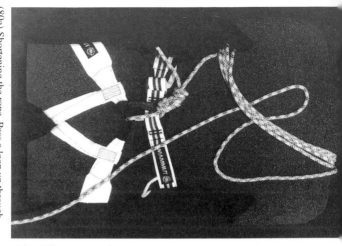

(80a) Shortening the rope. Pass a loop up through all the coils

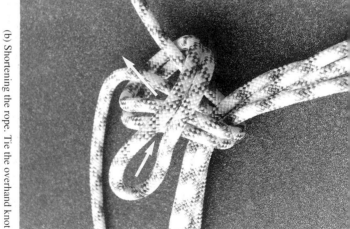

(b) Shortening the rope. Tie the overhand knot

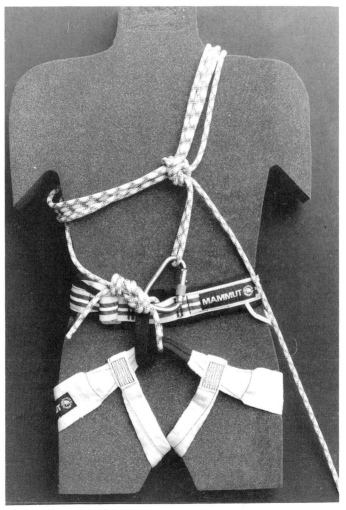

(81) Shortening the rope. The finished version

(82a) Carrying coils when moving together. Note that the 'live' rope can be released if required

(b) A method of locking off the coils

(c) Lap coiling. Not quite so easy to hold a load

climber.

On easy ground where it is possible to climb without using hands, it is as well to move quite close together – say 3–4 m (10–12 ft) apart – with the remainder of the rope carried by each climber. On slightly more difficult terrain or particularly on snow slopes you should only take coils on the rope that goes to the person below you. This affords a greater margin of safety when it comes to correcting a slip as the rope can be pulled tight immediately. There is no risk of them letting go of coils and thereby gaining speed and momentum in the fall. It goes without saying that the most experienced member of the party should be in the highest up the hill position. If for some reason this person slips you can only pray that they are able to stop themselves.

If the terrain requires the use of both hands you will most likely find it easier to move with the 10 m (30–35 ft) of rope out. In order to afford safety for both climbers the lead climber should put on running belays. These running belays may take the traditional form of a nut or a sling over a spike or a Friend or a piton. They could easily be the rope simply draped around a spike or a boulder or even just being on the opposite side of the ridge to your partner. These 'natural' running belays need to be treated with caution as sharp edges may cut the rope in the event of a fall. I recall a climb in New Zealand (not a recommended outing, I can tell you) where the rocks on the ridge were so sharp we moved together with the rope 'quadrupled' between us. If the lead climber continues to put on running belays in this way, he or she will soon run out and the person behind will be laden down with all the kit. So, from time to time you will need to meet up with your partner and either swap leads or swap equipment.

When you come across something difficult on the climb and you feel the need for greater security, it is a simple matter to arrange a more traditional belay. You may decide to use all of the rope or just a portion of it. Similarly you may decide to anchor yourself as in pitched climbing or use a direct belay which is probably more appropriate to the technique of moving together.

In either case it is quick to drop coils from your body to gain extra length. In some cases only one of the climbers need drop coils. It really depends on how much rope is required.

Direct belays (see page 174) play an important role in moving together techniques so it is well to practise until you are familiar with the different types of direct belay.

*Please note* that moving together does not afford the safety of traditional pitch climbing. One cannot hope to hold a serious leader fall or even, if they have the opportunity to gather momentum, a second falling for that matter. Safety lies in keeping the rope tight between each climber and being on the ball and quick enough to correct a slip before it turns into something a lot more serious.

## MOVING TOGETHER – THREE ON THE ROPE

The techniques are essentially the same as two on a rope. It is probably advisable that the middle person ties on without taking any coils. Also you should consider carefully how you tie the rope into the harness. The easiest way is to tie a figure of eight or an Alpine butterfly knot and clip it to the harness via a screwgate karabiner. However, there are some harnesses that do not function correctly or safely if you do this. The Whillans harness is one such example. With this harness you must tie in to the loops as per the manufacturer's recommendation. To tie into the harness take the portion of rope that you want to tie into and thread it (it will be doubled) through the tie in loops and tie a bowline knot treating the doubled rope as one rope. The resulting knot is terribly bulky but it is really the safest way of tying in. Incidentally, there is nothing to stop you from tying the middle of the rope into all harnesses this way (Photo 83).

Tying on to the middle of the rope often presents problems for that person. He or she can literally be torn between two climbers. To avoid this occurring it is advisable to tie the figure of eight or the Alpine butterfly with a long loop and then to tie

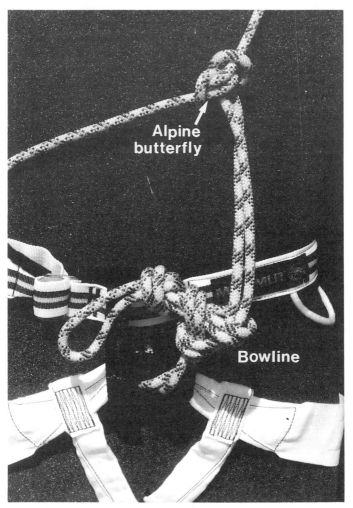

**Alpine butterfly**

**Bowline**

(83) Tying on to the middle of the rope using a bowline tied in
a loop of rope through the tie in loops of the harness

a figure of eight in the loop which is then clipped in to the harness (Photo 14). This then allows a certain amount of freedom of movement for the middle person. You should ensure that the distance between the harness and Alpine butterfly or figure of eight is such that it can never go out of arm's reach.

It is quite possible to have an infinite number of people on a rope thus, and keep on adding ropes and ropes, but sense and sensibility dictate that there must be a limit. I would venture to suggest that this be something like four or five to a rope on very easy ground and less as the terrain becomes more difficult. The exception to the rule is glacier travel, in which case the more the merrier for safety purposes. Glacier travel is dealt with under a separate heading for although it is still technically moving together, the specific techniques are a case apart.

## LEADER BRINGING TWO CLIMBERS UP AT THE SAME TIME

This technique is used quite often in guiding or instructional situations and is a fairly quick way of mixing traditional pitch technique with moving together. It can be used effectively by a team of three climbers where movement up the climb would otherwise be a slow and tedious process. If used efficiently there is no reason why three shouldn't move almost as quickly as two. The lead climber should of course be experienced enough to be able to handle bringing two climbers up at the same time. Traditional anchoring methods are relevant but obviously one needs to consider the fact that you may have to hold both climbers at the same time, so make sure that anchors are good.

The method of belaying should also be given careful consideration. A body belay such as the waist or shoulder belay is not enough. It should be a belay plate or similar device or possibly an Italian hitch. Whatever system you decide to use the rope to each of the climbers you are safeguarding must operate independently of the other. An Italian hitch in both ropes together,

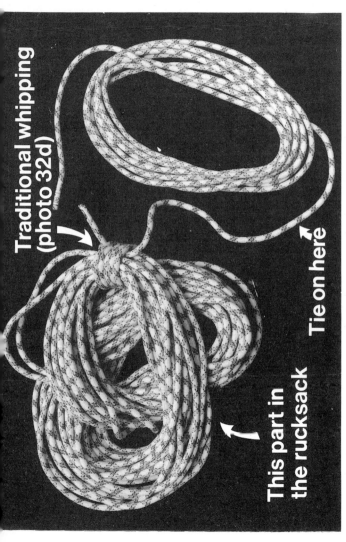

Traditional whipping
(photo 32d)

This part in
the rucksack

Tie on here

(84) Shortening the rope to carry the bulk of it in a rucksack

clipped into one krab will not work efficiently.

The two climbers, rather than climb side by side, should move about 5 m (15 ft) apart, one behind the other. They should be tied into clearly identifiable ropes so that the belayer is aware of who's doing what at any time. On difficult or serious terrain it may not be practical to bring both climbers up at the same time. An advantage of this system is that it is convenient to revert to traditional pitched climbing at any time and use the moving together technique on easier or less serious ground. When belaying the leader either of the 'seconds' may take on the task or both could belay the leader on their own ropes.

## Other Methods of Shortening the Rope

In other situations, for example if you only want to safeguard a less experienced or more cautious companion over a short tricky section of a climb, it would be laborious and unnecessary to go through the previous procedure.

Photo 84 shows a method where only a part of the rope is used and the remainder stored in the rucksack. This will obviously cause problems if you discover that you need more rope than you have instantly available, so be sure that you have enough to hand. Never just 'stuff' the spare rope in your rucksack as I can guarantee you will snag it somehow and pull it all out of the pack.

There are a couple of other ways of tying off the rope as well as the one described, but so long as the rope is tied off neatly and securely it doesn't really matter how it's done.

# Glacier Travel

Glacier travel is an important aspect of Alpine mountaineering. The most serious part of an Alpine climb is often the approach up a glacier or the descent at the end of the day. It is an aspect of mountaineering that is all too often taken lightly and without due regard to safety – until you fall into a crevasse – and then it becomes apparent that the words of caution were not spoken lightly.

Glaciers, like climbs, can be easy or complicated and difficult to negotiate. There is however no system of categorizing the difficulty of glacier travel, nor indeed would it be practical to do so. What one week may be a straightforward stroll, a week later could be a complicated mass of yawning crevasses and hungry crevasse tigers. It is not within the remit of this book to discuss the mountaineering skills of route-finding, suffice to say in these pages that glacier travel and its associated dangers should be treated with the utmost respect.

Before you decide on a method of roping up for glacier travel, it may be as well to consider the prerequisites. The rope is required for the safety of the party in negotiating crevassed areas where the dangers may not be visually apparent but may well result in a fall into a crevasse. In many cases a fall into a crevasse is only up to the chest level and extrication is a simple matter. If, however, you are crossing a large snow bridge and it collapses you may end up hanging well below the lip of the crevasse – maybe even dangling in space. You may also sustain an injury on the way down or be knocked unconscious. In just about every case you almost certainly lose contact with your companions on the surface. The rope must therefore be attached to the climber in such a way that it affords safety to someone falling into a crevasse *and* that it is possible for those who remain on the surface first to hold and later to secure and rescue any climber from a crevasse. There are numerous methods of tying on to the rope, some of which will be discussed here and others

(85) Every which way but loose! Glacier travel through complex terrain

that I propose to leave to self discovery.

To begin with let us consider the choice of harness. By far the most commonly used in mountaineering is the sit harness. Whilst such a harness is adequate for nearly all climbing scenarios, any of which might result in a fallen climber hanging free with a heavy rucksack on their back, it may cause the climber to tip upside down and even fall out of the harness. For this reason I recommend that you give careful thought to the type of harness used in Alpine mountaineering and if for you a full body harness is not a worthwhile buy, that you consider using a chest harness, improvised or otherwise, and connect it to the sit harness. There are a number of lightweight and efficient chest harnesses available and one such is shown in Photo 86b. A two-piece system such as this allows the climber the choice of sit or full body harness applicable to whatever they may be doing. The sequence of photographs shows a way to use the rope to connect the two together (Photos 86a and b).

Generally speaking you should move on a glacier with about 8–10 m (25–30 ft) of rope between each climber in much the same way as the moving together techniques already described (page 178). This allows a good margin of safety for holding a falling climber and also enough rope for exploratory probing. Anything more than this can lead to tangles and confusion and anything less lowers the safety margins. It is, however, important to remember that unlike other methods of moving together, you must *not* at any time carry coils in the hand.

The basis of the safety system lies in keeping the rope tight between the climbers at all times. By allowing slack to develop you increase the length of any fall and decrease your chances of success in holding someone securely. The minimum safe number of climbers on a rope is obviously two. Obviously, the more climbers on the rope the greater the margins of safety and the greater the likelihood of stopping someone should they fall into a crevasse. The longest 'rope' of climbers I have ever seen was about 73 – it was difficult to keep count! This was on the Tour

(86a) Connecting a sit harness to a chest harness

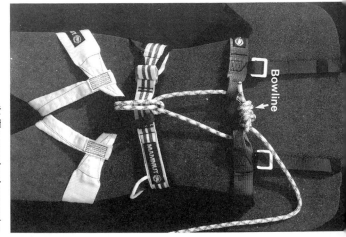

(b) The completed connection

Glacier in Chamonix.

Regardless of the number of climbers on the rope it is important to ensure that there is sufficient spare rope in the party to effect a rescue. This can be carried in coils around the body or in the rucksack or you might even have a complete spare rope in your pack.

In theory, the 'safest' position on the rope in glacier travel is in between two other climbers. Here you have a rope from both sides so the chances of being stopped before you fall too far are quite high – provided of course that your companions are alert. It is quite possible that you could spend a lifetime travelling over glaciers and not fall into anything serious that requires complex rescue procedures. But it is such an unknown quantity that it would be foolish to become complacent. At all times you must be 'on the ball' and ready to hold a fall.

## ROPING-UP TECHNIQUES

### Two on the Rope

For two climbers moving on a glacier you should rope-up, as I said before, about 8–10 m (25–30 ft) apart. Use the middle of the rope leaving on a 45 m (150 ft) rope, for example, about 18 m (60 ft) at either end. This spare rope is then coiled around the body in the way shown in Photos 80 and 81. The coils must be tied of in the manner illustrated. This method of tying on has the advantage that it creates a chest support which is particularly effective if the coils are reasonably snug around the shoulder. In the event of a fall, the initial impact is taken on the sit harness and the coils support the upper body.

You should always put a 'prusik' loop on the rope. I recommend that this be the longest of the loops that you have so that if you do fall down a crevasse you do at least have something that you can stand in immediately. You will find this important from the point of view of comfort. Whilst walking along the glacier the spare cord can be tucked in the pocket or tied loosely to the harness.

For reasons that will soon become apparent use a Klemheist knot and tie a figure of eight knot in the sling about halfway along. This is then used as a handle to assist with keeping the rope out from under your feet and more importantly to help hold a falling companion (page 203). The leading climber is the one at most risk of falling into a crevasse. But don't think that you're excused the pleasure just by being at the back! For the people behind the leader the Klemheist can be used as a handle to assist you with holding a fall and it is also a convenient knot to use when the time comes to secure the rope prior to rescuing a companion from a crevasse (see Crevasse Rescue page 201).

When moving over the glacier keep the rope taut at all times, particularly when there are route-finding difficulties and the leading climber is probing for hidden crevasses. If necessary, you should not hesitate to use a temporary belay of some kind (see page 103) to safeguard each other over difficult or danger-ous snow bridges.

## Three or More on a Rope

I would suggest that four climbers would be the maximum number you should consider tying into one 45 m (150 ft) or 50 m (165 ft) length of rope. This allows for about 9 m (30 ft) of rope between each person and about 9 m (30 ft) spare at either end for effecting rescues. You may of course have a whole rope spare in a party of four climbers which can be used to work on a rescue. The people in the 'middle' of the rope could tie on in the manner recommended on page 184. Give careful considera-tion to whether or not these people should be tied into a full body harness, improvised or otherwise. My suggestion is that they should be, but, as there is much less chance of them falling a long way into a crevasse it is possible to get away with wear-ing a sit harness. It is, however such a simple matter to rig an improvised chest harness which will at least provide some sup-port, that you may be foolhardy not to do so. Photo 87 shows a

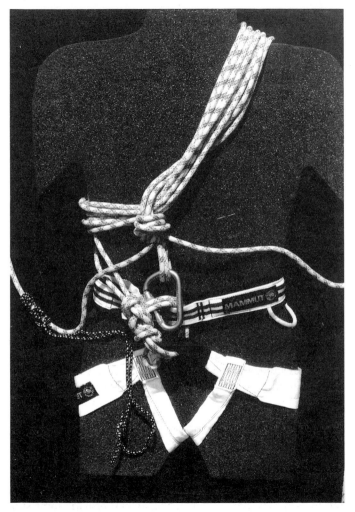

(87) Tying on to the middle of the rope using coils for chest support

method of making an improvised chest harness from the rope. Each 'middle' person should put a prusik loop on the rope to the climber in front of them. This can then be used as a handle to assist with holding the person in front of you.

Do not become complacent with regard to safety. Just because there is safety in numbers, it doesn't mean you're exempt from the experience of falling into a crevasse. Keep the rope taut at all times and *don't* carry coils.

## SAFETY WHEN NEGOTIATING DIFFICULTIES

### Snow bridges

If you should come across a seemingly weak or a narrow snow bridge it is important that each climber be safeguarded across. It is not enough to casually stroll along and hope that nothing will happen. Often it may be safety enough that the person behind keeps the rope very tight and moves forward only as the one crossing the bridge needs rope. All other people on the rope should keep the rope tight and be similarly braced. Once one person is across this procedure can be repeated for the remainder of the party. Make sure though that you keep the party strung out and don't gather together in one spot. It has happened that parties have grouped together over a crevasse and the whole thing has collapsed depositing everyone in the hole.

If you feel the need for a more solid form of anchor you may choose to make one of the snow anchors described in the section on snow and ice anchors. It would be true to say however, that in the majority of cases keeping the rope tight is more than adequate.

### Jumping a Crevasse

Jumping over crevasses, whilst testing your long jump skills, can be a dangerous thing to do. It is often necessary though, and you would be as well to bear a few things in mind. Firstly ensure that the person jumping has enough rope to make the distance! That sounds a bit obvious but I have witnessed a few occasions where there hasn't been enough rope and either the person jumping was pulled back into the crevasse or the next person on the rope had to make a hurried decision to jump. Make sure that you have as good a take off as possible and that the landing is fairly safe. Jumping downhill is the most risky because it is often difficult to control the momentum. If you have someone who is a little nervous about jumping you can wait for them to jump and, if you don't think that they are going to make it, assist them by pulling on the rope! It works, just so long as you don't pull before they jump.

You may decide that you need a more secure anchor and belay in which case use an appropriate system from the chapter on anchors on snow, rock and ice.

## Crossing a Bergschrund

Depending on the size of the bergschrund you have to cross, it is likely that you will treat this aspect of mountaineering as a 'pitched' climb. You may not rig-up the anchors as you would do in a fully fledged pitch situation but you will certainly move one at a time.

In ascent, having chosen the crossing point, the leader will go across. He or she will be belayed by the next person along the rope. This could once more, be a simple matter of keeping the rope taut. In descent, again depending on the size of the beast, it is probably better to gather together at a convenient position above the bergschrund and rig up a belay. Try to make sure that you have a fairly comfortable stance. This may mean hacking out a large platform to stand on or if the climb you are on is fairly popular the stance will probably be large enough.

The leader or most experienced member of the party will probably go last. All other members may be lowered down or they may climb to safety. If there is room it is a good idea for all the party to spread out along the length of rope available and keep it taut to afford extra safety. The last person over the 'schrund' is protected by all the others keeping the rope respectably taut – though not so tight that you run the risk of pulling the person off. Should the leader discover that the bergschrund is straightforward enough to cross without resorting to belaying each member, the party can resume a moving together technique and treat the obstacle just like another crevasse.

Occasionally it will be necessary to abseil over a bergschrund. Try, if possible, to do this near to some rocks and you may be able to use a rock anchor. If there is no rock anchor available you will either have to abseil off a bollard – the most likely – or an ice screw or a retrievable T-axe. (See chapters Anchors on Snow and Ice and Other Useful Rope Tricks.)

At risk of repeating myself, I would like to reiterate the importance of good rope management and a sensible approach to glacier travel. Too often one is witness to sloppy technique and accidents, including deaths, that could so easily have been avoided.

# Crevasse Rescue

'To come down a glacier without relaxing the essential precautions asks, in most cases, for a special and sustained effort of will. It is usually done in the afternoon; the party is tired; the snow is softening in the warm sun; the hard climb is over and everyone is relaxed; it is easy to be careless. This, above all, is the time when people fall into crevasses. It may sound strange but it happens again and again. The leader is sinking knee-deep into soft snow; the second man, hot and exhausted, full of the wish to be off the glacier as soon as possible, closes up to the leader; the third man is bored by walking alone and closes up to the second; their ropes trail behind them. Then someone goes through.'

From *On Climbing* by Sir Charles Evans, Museum Press, 1956.

Salutary words indeed, but so true.

This chapter deals with the techniques of getting out of a crevasse. Many of the techniques have already been discussed and it is simply a matter of putting them in context and discussing where and what will work best. As with all self-rescue situations, no two are ever the same. The circumstances are nearly always different; the time of day, the seriousness of the terrain, the abilities of individuals concerned and so it goes on. Armed with a repertoire of techniques however, the mountaineer can usually effect a rescue.

## THE BASIC CREVASSE RESCUE

The most common 'fall' into a crevasse is going through up to the waist or chest at the worst. Extraction is largely a matter of self preservation. That is to say, as soon as you feel your feet kicking around in space and that void below you, some strange power takes over and you're no sooner in than you're out. With a little help from your friends of course.

The serious problems begin when you are below ground level. Provided that your partner or partners have been doing their job well and the rope has been kept tight, you shouldn't fall too far into the crevasse. However, as soon as you go below ground level the rope will cut into the snow on the edge of the crevasse and this will give most of the problems.

To stop someone who is falling into a crevasse, the first thing you must do is fall to the ground and try to dig your feet in. There will probably be a few micro-seconds when you think you're not going to be able to hold but it is usually surprisingly easy, particularly if the rope cuts deep into the edge and creates a lot of friction. If you are the one who has fallen in and are literally only just below the surface, you may be able to get out with a struggle and a fair amount of tugging from your partners. If despite all the tugging and heaving and pushing, the rope remains stuck fast and you don't pop out, you must adopt a slightly more scientific approach. The climber, on the surface may decide to secure you to an anchor and come to the edge to help you. If there are three or more climbers on the rope, you can be held by the second person along while a third comes to your aid. Whoever it is that goes to the edge, they must make sure that they have some kind of protection just in case they fall through too. This will mean rigging an anchor for the second person, and then the third can go to the edge with the protection of a prusik loop on the loaded rope. This can be moved along as the climber approaches the edge.

When the rescuer gets to the edge the first thing to do is to put something, such as a spare ice axe, ski poles or rucksack, under the rope to try to prevent it from cutting deeper into the crevasse edge. After that it is possible to cut away a little of the edge in order to reveal the buried rope. *Take care* when hacking the snow away from around the loaded rope because the slightest touch may well be enough to cut it. Remember, a loaded rope cuts very easily. You should have a very good chance of getting out once all that has been done, without having to resort to complicated pulley systems and hoists.

### The 'Real' Thing!

If despite careful ropework or because of a lack of attention, a climber disappears well below the surface, you will have something more serious to deal with. One of the problems confronting you from the outset will be the lack of ability to communicate between surface and crevasse and this will frustrate attempts at rescue. It is important that you establish with all of the party, before you go out in the mountains, exactly what will happen if one of the group falls deeply into a crevasse. This will speed up the rescue procedure because at least everyone has an idea of what is going on, including, most importantly, the person down the crevasse.

As a general rule, once someone has fallen into a crevasse the person on the surface should rig up an anchor and escape from the system. Meanwhile the person in the crevasse should, provided they are able, make sure that they have their prusiks on the rope. They will almost certainly have one, but may not have the other on so do that immediately. At the same time try to take stock of the situation and decide the best way to get out of the hole.

When escaping from the system on the surface, life is made much more straightforward by having a prusik loop already on the rope. If you use, as suggested in the previous chapter, a Klemheist in the long prusik loop, it is a simple matter to convert it to a French prusik autobloc. Photos 88, 89 and 90 show the sequence of escaping from the system 'crevasse rescue' style. The escape can be effected in much the same way as it is done on a rock climb. Refer to the appropriate pages for more detail. The procedure is as follows.

Take the strain of the fallen person by immediately dropping to the ground and digging your feet in. Once you have stopped sliding and your partner falling you have to try to get an anchor in. This could be any of the snow anchors described in the chapter on snow, rock and ice anchors, but remember that the snow may be very soft and unpredictable.

If there are more than two of you on the rope, it is preferable to get someone behind you to rig the anchor. You would do well not to underestimate the difficulty of holding someone's weight while trying to arrange an anchor. Having rigged the anchor, you must then convert the Klemheist to a French prusik, as in Photo 88 and clip it into the anchor. Having done that move forward gradually to take all the weight off yourself and transfer it to the anchor. That done you can untie all the coils from around you and untie completely. Make sure that you tie the rope into the anchor with a separate krab before doing anything else. This is your safety back-up in the event that the autobloc fails (Photo 90).

As soon as you have escaped from the system you must try to establish contact with the person down the crevasse. To do this you will need to go to the edge of the crevasse. It would be sensible to approach the edge of the crevasse very cautiously and

(88) Escaping the system during crevasse rescue – stage one

(89) Having rigged your anchor, convert the Klemheist to a French prusik and clip it to the anchor – stage two

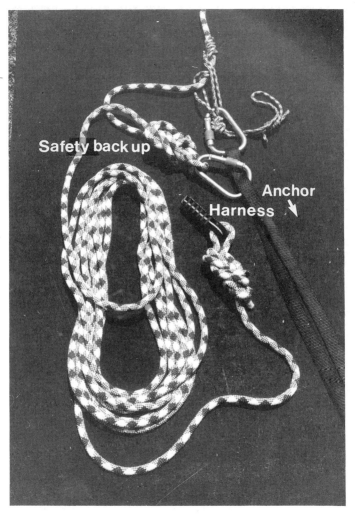

(90) The final stage. The escape complete you can now rescue the victim

on hands and knees with a prusik loop on the load rope or some other safety device attached to the anchor. This of course could be a spare rope or the remaining rope that was coiled around your shoulder. Once on the edge, put some padding or something under the rope to prevent it cutting any deeper into the crevasse edge.

When you have established communication you can decide, between the two of you, on the best course of action. It may be that the person down the crevasse decides to prusik out. If so, you will need to sort out the edge of the crevasse so that it is easier for the crevasse bound climber to get out. This will certainly involve plenty of hacking away at the edge and a deluge of snow down onto the victim. If you are unable to clear away the snow from around the loaded rope the best thing to do is to cut a box-shaped slot just to the side of where the rope has cut in. You could then drop a spare bit of rope down this to help the victim get over the very awkward final edge. This can be used to pull the victim out or for them to transfer to when they arrive near the top.

If you are the person that has to prusik out you will find it easier to do so without a rucksack on. As you begin to ascend you will notice that a loop of slack rope develops. This loop will get longer the higher you go. As soon as you can identify this loop, take off your rucksack and clip it into the loop so that it hangs below you. If you have skis on you can dangle them from this loop too. Be careful not to drop any equipment!

The party may decide that an assisted hoist (page 154) is the answer to the problems. In which case set the ropes up for the hoist in the way illustrated in Photo 69 but you need not put on the belay plate of course. The biggest problem you will encounter here is getting the hoisting loop down to the victim. Once achieved however, extraction is a simple matter – well, fairly simple. Never discount the possibility that the person who has fallen down the hole might be able to walk out out along a snow bridge if lowered down a short distance.

## Dealing with Problems

The most likely problem to occur is that the rope will have cut so deeply into the edge of the crevasse that it is completely jammed. In this event you will be unable to use it to aid the rescue. If the victim decides to prusik out, he or she should do so on this rope up to the point that it disappears into the edge. Meanwhile the people on the surface should rig up a second rope for the victim to transfer to for the final stage out.

If you have to do a hoist, assisted or otherwise, a slightly different approach to that previously described is required. Escape as illustrated in Photos 88–90 and go to the edge to cut a box shaped slot just to the side of the jammed rope. Make sure that you arrange something to prevent the rope from cutting deeper into the edge. Go back to the anchor and fix a second figure of eight knot in the rope and clip it into the anchor. If you have a spare sling then use this as it will become much less complicated around the anchor attachment (Photo 91). To all intents and purposes, the rope that originally held the victim becomes redundant, although at this stage their weight is still hanging on it.

Using the rope from the second figure of eight knot that you tied, drop a loop with a pulley attached, down to the victim. This is then clipped into the victim's harness at a secure place – preferably the central loop. If for some reason this loop is not long enough to reach the victim, it can be extended with a sling. The slack end of the rope is passed through an Alpine clutch or through a karabiner and pulley with a French prusik autobloc. On this rope and between the autobloc and the victim put on a short prusik loop. Take the rope from the other side of the autobloc and clip it to this prusik (Photo 90). By pulling on the rope indicated in the photo you should be able to hoist your victim. The victim can actually help a little by pulling on the rope that is attached to the second figure of eight knot that you tied earlier on. Once the load comes off the original holding rope a third person could, if desired, undo the figure of eight back-up, convert it to an Italian

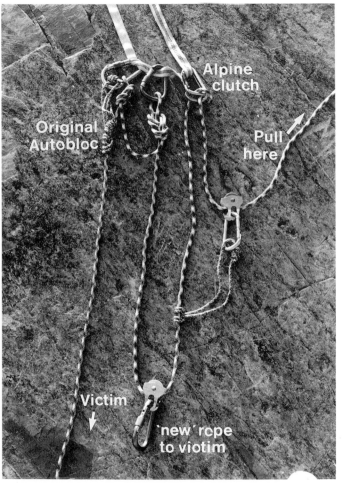

(91) Crevasse rescue if the main rope is jammed in the edge of the crevasse

hitch and take in the rope as the victim gains height.

*Unconscious Victim*

If the person who falls down the crevasse is injured or has been knocked unconscious, you will have very different problems to solve. Without doubt, the first thing to do is to go down to the victim and take stock of the situation. It may be necessary to administer First Aid. You must make sure that the anchor you have placed is strong enough to take the weight of two people. Invariably this will mean backing the original up with a second anchor or creating a new one just for the rescuer.

You will then probably have to hoist the victim to the surface. This in itself is a difficult and onerous task and not one to be undertaken lightly. It is tempting to say glibly here that you should go to the surface and rig up an unassisted hoist as illustrated in Photo 72 but in truth if you are on your own you have very little hope of being able to pull an unconscious victim to the surface. It is difficult enough even with two or three people. There is, however enough information in these chapters to give you a chance of rescuing an unconscious person but don't expect to be able to do it without some practice first – and certainly don't expect it to be easy.

Remember that small pulleys – such as those manufactured by Petzl – reduce friction. If none are available use double krabs to reduce the angle of the turn at each moving part of the system.

## Hints on Practising Crevasse Rescue

Many people practise the techniques of crevasse extraction on a dry glacier i.e. one that is bare ice and where all the crevasses are visible. This is quite a good starting point to pick up the basics but it is not terribly realistic. It is much better to go to some real crevasses on a snow covered glacier to practise. You should be able to make everything perfectly safe by having back-up anchors for everything so that if someone fails to hold a falling

**Victim**

**Safety rope whilst practising**

(92) Making an anchor whilst holding someone who has fallen in a crevasse. In this case a T–axe is used

(93) Crossing a narrow snow bridge. The rope is taut in both directions

climber at least they are not all going to fall in.

I would suggest this as a worthwhile exercise as it gives you a more realistic idea of what to expect and, in my experience, makes you aware of the importance of not being too relaxed on a glacier. You need not even go to a glacier to practise. Small cornices or other features in the British hills in winter provide a similar formation to a crevasse. Please make sure that the 'run out' is perfectly safe – the top of Number 5 Gully on Ben Nevis would certainly not be ideal!

# Other Useful Rope 'Tricks'

In this final chapter I propose to discuss a few techniques that didn't seem to fit in under any other headings but are, nevertheless, appropriate to a rope techniques book. The first two techniques are often labelled as pretty fancy tricks for instructors and guides only but this needn't be the case at all. Admittedly, they have limited use and sometimes don't work. Nonetheless, if they are set up correctly and with some thought, there will be occasions when you might find them useful.

## RETRIEVABLE ICE SCREW

This trick will only work reliably with tubular screw in/screw out ice screws. The ice screw must not be too long and you must also make sure that the cord used to activate the retrieval is long enough to unscrew the ice screw completely. Photo 94 show the set-up in the ice ready for abseiling and the method for setting it up. The Penberthy knot must be attached to the rope that you are going to pull. If, therefore, you are abseiling on two ropes joined put the Penberthy just above the joining knot. The cord that initiates the turning of the screw must always be attached to the left hand rope. If it is attached to the right it will only tighten the screw into the ice! You could arrange the connection of ice screw to rope by using a piece of cord or tape and tying it into an overhand loop in the abseil rope. This works just as well as the method illustrated. When you put in the ice screw it is worthwhile unscrewing it and screwing it back in a couple of times to ensure that it will unscrew easily. This is particularly necessary if it is many degrees below freezing as the screw could freeze in tighter whilst you are abseiling.

## RETRIEVABLE ICE AXE

A similar sort of gimmick to the retrievable ice screw but

Penberthy

(94) Retrievable ice screw

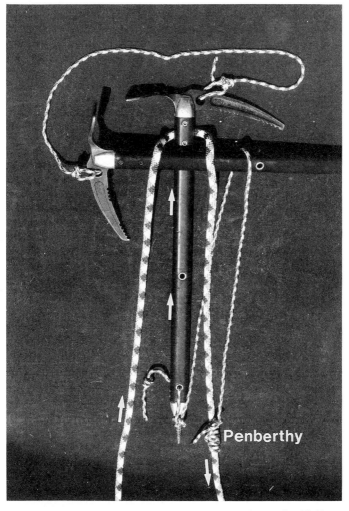

(95) Retrievable T-axe

nonetheless one that I know has been put to good use on a number
of occasions, particularly abseiling over bergschrunds. Photo 95
shows the method for setting it up.

There are some important considerations to take into account. Firstly, the snow that you set the anchor up in must be
fairly solid and reliable. When you are arranging the T-axe in the
slot make sure that the vertical axe will run smoothly up and
down the hole. The slot that you cut for the rope to run through
should be a little wider than what you would cut for a normal
T-axe anchor. This is to allow the rope to run more smoothly.
Make sure that the cord that you use for the Penberthy knot at one
end and the attachment to the spike of the vertical axe at the other,
is quite long. The vertical axe must be pulled completely clear of
the snow before the connection to the horizontal axe comes tight.
Stand very well clear of the rope when you do retrieve the
equipment! When pulling try to get the vertical axe out in one
movement and keep up the momentum so that it pulls the
horizontal one out with it.

## TENSIONING ROPES FOR TYROLEANS AND OTHER AERIAL ROPEWAYS

There are probably few occasions in day to day climbing when
you will need to tension ropes. However, if you are involved in
taking people – youngsters or adults – into the outdoors, you will
probably find yourself setting up death slides, Postman's Walks,
Tyroleans and a whole manner of ropeway adventures.

The first such adventure I had was on my introduction to
Rock climbing course run by Pete Crew and Al Harris from
Wendy's Cafe in Llanberis. We had gone to Gogarth for the day
climbing and having just endured a Harris boulder trundling
session, whilst I was still at water level, we wandered over to
Wen Zawn. Within a short space of time two ropes, knotted
together were stretched across the Zawn from the top of Wen
crack to the promontory down below. The knot was almost

(c) Tying off the rope using a series of half hitches

(b) 'Marrying' the ropes to prevent slippage while tying off to the anchor

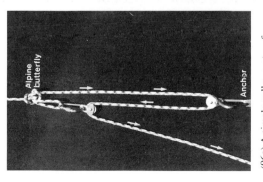

(96a) A simple pulley system for tensioning a rope

exactly halfway along. My only recollection of this adventure is of desperately trying to get past the knot without falling into the sea which was swirling and splashing and roaring what felt like thousands of feet below me. I've never done that tyrolean since!

One of the problems with setting up such a system with climbing ropes is that in order to get a good slide and the right amount of tightness in the rope, it is necessary to tension the ropes until all the stretch has been taken out. The strength of a climbing rope lies in its ability to absorb the shock of a falling climber. Taking all of the stretch out of the rope before you subject it to a load is putting the strain on it when it is at its weakest. This is surely not a good thing. On many occasions I have witnessed teams of ten or more people heaving on a climbing rope to get it guitar string tight and then bouncing about, see-sawing back and forth and generally subjecting it to forces that surely one day will cause their demise.

If you are involved in such activities on a regular basis you would be advised to buy a low- or non-stretch abseil rope specifically for such adventures. It is not then necessary to tension the ropes to near breaking point before you can use them. In fact it only requires a couple of people to set up. Not only that but the ropes themselves are much more durable.

Photos 96a, b and c show a tensioning system applicable to all aerial ropeways. Note that pulleys have been used at each turn in the rope. Every time you put a turn in the rope you are weakening it to a certain extent – the tighter the turn the weaker the rope. By putting pulleys at each turn the diameter of turn is much less and therefore weakens the system less. Once you have the right amount of tension in the rope and you want to secure it, get someone to hold the ropes as illustrated in Photo 96b. This is called 'marrying the ropes' and is a simple and effective way to ensure that you don't let any of the rope slip back through whilst tying it off. From time to time you will need to retension the ropes to keep them at the desired level of tightness. This is a simple matter. The tie off at the anchor can easily be undone even when under load.

Frontispiece: Well prepared for an MIA assessment!

Nigel Shepherd

# Further modern rope techniques

*with special information for SPA & MIA*

Constable · London

Rock climbing, ice climbing and other aspects of mountaineering are inherently dangerous and the techniques described in this book require considerable practice before they can be implemented safely and efficiently on crag and mountain. The techniques require careful judgement, which can only be based on long experience.

We strongly advise that anyone wishing to practice the techniques described herein should do so under the expert tuition of a qualified professional and must recognise the risks that are involved and personally accept the responsibility associated with those risks.

# Contents

# List of Illustrations

# Acknowledgements

Whilst the words in this book are entirely my own, I cannot claim full credit for the information offered.

The topics discussed are so diverse in character and there are so many differing ways to do things that it is sometimes difficult to stand back from the task in hand to obtain a realistic and unbiased overview of the work. To this end I am indebted to many, but particularly to Nick Banks and Steve Long who kindly gave of their time to read through the manuscript; to Graham MacMahon who was always incredibly enthusiastic about bouncing ideas around and came up with a host of useful suggestions and who helped with some of the pictures – he probably wished he didn't live so close by; to Martin Atkinson of Wild Country who very kindly donated all of the gear used in the photographs; to Mark, Wyn and David at Cambrian Photography in Colwyn Bay who patiently answered an endless barrage of questions and offered kindly advice.

# 1 The SPA, MIA and MIC

There have been instructor awards in this country for more than five decades. In the very beginning the Mountaineering Association employed instructors and gave them an in-house qualification. This led eventually to the introduction of the Mountaineering Instructor Certificate (MIC) (now the Mountain Instructor Certificate) and the Advanced certificate (MIAC). During the formative years of the qualifications there were very few active professional instructors who earned their living entirely by their trade – quite the reverse of today!

The Mountain Leaders Certificate (now the Mountain Leader Award) followed on, bridging the gap between those who wanted only to take walking groups into the hills and those wishing to become involved in rock climbing.

During the 1970s Outdoor Pursuits Centres proliferated throughout the country and alongside this growth it was inevitable that there would be a vast increase in the number of full time instructors. Gradually the demand for qualification increased.

The origins of the Single Pitch Award (SPA), originally called the Single Pitch Supervisors Award (SPSA) but changed when the Scottish Mountain Leader Training Board joined the scheme, go back to the early 1980s. At this time there were a number of people working in outdoor activities who identified a need for some sort of measure of competence for those taking groups onto crags and who introduce others to the sport of rock climbing. A number of local authority schemes were already in operation but it was felt that something nationally recognised was required. The BMC Training Committee deliberated long and hard about the direction they should take and at the conclusion of discussions it was decided to publish simple guidelines on what should be considered good and safe practice on single pitch rock climbing venues.

For many this was an unsatisfactory state of affairs and, though it fulfilled part of an obligation, it didn't quite go far enough. In 1992 the newly formed UKMTB established a training and certification programme specifically targeted at those taking groups on to single pitch rock climbing venues. From the outset it was envisaged that this would be a very basic qualification, attainable by anyone who has a genuine interest in and a commitment to the sport of rock climbing and who gives time over to introduce others to the sport – for financial reward or otherwise

Around the same time the MIC underwent considerable changes. The most far reaching of these was to split the qualification into two separate components. The Mountain Instructor Award is aimed at those who wish to instruct mountaineering skills in summer only and the Mountain Instructor Certificate is an add-on for those who also wish to instruct winter climbing skills. Prior to these changes being introduced the award of the MIC was only attainable by those with considerable experience in both summer and winter disciplines. The flood gates opened and within a few years more than 500 people registered for the MIA scheme, thus proving a need and at the same time satisfying the demand.

This brief historical perspective is important to understanding the differences between the various qualifications and putting the skills of ropework into some kind of comprehensible perspective. Whilst some techniques will undoubtedly cross over from one qualification to the other, it should be made clear that the levels of competence required to attain each award are significantly different, as is the experience of the participant.

The syllabus of the SPA is intended to offer training and qualification for those who wish to instruct on single pitch climbing venues only. The definition of single pitch is any crag that is:

- climbed without intermediate stances
- described as a single pitch in the guidebook
- allows students to be lowered to the ground at all times
- is non-tidal
- is non-serious and has little objective danger
- presents no difficulties on approach or retreat, such as route finding, scrambling or navigation.

As part of their assessment candidates are required to demonstrate their ability to lead on Severe grade rock and to be able to place sound running belays and to arrange a good stance at the top of the climb. This requirement ensures that all those undertaking the scheme are committed rock climbers and have a good understanding of the sport.

Candidates are also assessed on their ability to solve problems. These are in general very straightforward and will not involve complex rope manoeuvres or major cliff evacuations.

A part of the scheme is dedicated to climbing wall use and the supervision of groups. Many climbing walls now require anyone bringing a group for instruction to have the SPA as a minimum level of competence. This is a reliable yardstick and reassures the management that those under supervision are being well looked after.

The MIA is an altogether more comprehensive award. In addition to the skills required for the SPA, candidates for this scheme are required to demonstrate their ability to take care of and instruct on multi-pitch climbs up to Very Severe standard. The teaching element also includes the ability to instruct students in the skills of leading and the complexities of safe ropework. They will also be asked to solve much more complex rescue scenarios that may require multi pitch evacuation of the cliff with an injured climber.

The award also requires that they be competent to lead people on scrambling terrain, either as a day out in its own right, part of a mountain day or when the techniques of short roping are required in descent from a rock climb.

The MIC is an add-on component to the MIA and successful completion of this allows instructors to instruct and lead in winter conditions, including climbs up to Grade III standard.

Beyond these qualifications is that of Mountain Guide. To achieve this award candidates must be experienced and competent mountaineers in every respect. They will be required to demonstrate their ability to teach and guide to a high standard, both in the UK in all seasons and in the Alps, both on foot and on ski.

There are very clear differences between all the awards in terms of what is required of candidates. A common thread binds them – that whatever rope technique is required must be used competently and safely, there is no allowable margin of error when you are responsible for people's well-being and enjoyment.

# 2 Top Roping and Bottom Roping

On single pitch climbing venues you will either choose to safeguard those in your care from the top of the crag or to have the rope doubled through an anchor at the top of the crag and belay climbers from the bottom.

Each method has its merits and for that matter, its drawbacks. If you have a group to take out for the day, belaying from the bottom of the crag will enable you, as the instructor, to keep more people actively involved for more of the time. It is possible to arrange two or three climbs to take place simultaneously and you flit backwards and forwards between each group making sure that each is conducted safely. If you belay from the top of the crag it is very unlikely that you will be able to entertain more than one novice climber at a time.

Using a bottom rope belaying system means that you can allow the group to belay each other. Whilst one of them is climbing, two or three others can be responsible for belaying. Thus two climbs might conceivably actively involve up to eight people at any one time. There is much to be said in favour of this, not least that everyone will feel a part of the activity by working together, and they are much less likely to lose interest.

The major drawback with the technique of bottom roping is that it has a profound effect on the environment by concentrating a large number of people in one place, causing considerable erosion to both the rock and to the ground immediately below a climb. It is also rather invasive, limiting access to the routes that you are using for others who may wish to climb them. You should always be considerate in your use of the crags and allow others to climb the routes that you are on by vacating them as quickly as possible.

In such a situation you, as the instructor, will have an

enormous responsibility to ensure that everything is done safely and that no-one gets hurt by tomfoolery or neglect or carelessness. To organise two climbs at the same time you must choose routes that are close enough together that it takes only a second or two for you to move from one to the other. In that way you are more likely to be able to keep control of the situation. To have three climbs on the go at the same time is much more difficult to manage and with complete beginners may not be practicable nor, indeed, advisable.

## RIGGING ANCHORS

In order to set up a bottom roping system you will first need to go to the top of the crag and arrange the anchor points. It is very important to ensure that the anchors are solid. Unless it is a big stout tree, firmly established, or a large purpose-designed anchor, it is preferable to select more than one anchor.

One anchor point is only suitable if the climb is immediately below it and any load from below will be directed straight on to the anchor. If there is the slightest chance that a falling climber will swing off to one side, two anchor points (minimum) will be needed in order to stabilise the direction of pull. Such simplistic situations are unfortunately rare and it is more common to find that anchor points are well off to the side of where you would like them to be.

You will need to have the fixing point of the climbing rope draped over the edge of the crag. The ideal that you should strive for is to arrange things so that the climber does not have to go over the top of the crag but can climb up until they can just touch the karabiner that secures their safety rope. From that moment the belayers can take the weight of the climber and lower him or her back down to the bottom of the crag.

It is therefore necessary to have anchors that are well back from the edge and to use a rope to connect them all to one central point which is then draped over the top of the crag. If the only suitable anchors are to be found close to the edge it is better to set up the bottom roping system so that the end of the climb is well out of arm's reach of the anchor points.

When you construct an anchor point in this way, the position at which the climbing rope is attached may be subjected to considerable movement across the rock. If you do not take account of this the rope could very quickly become chaffed and worn through to the extent that it is damaged beyond further use. Similarly, the rope that is used for climbing on may be subjected to the same chaffing effect. There is a need to keep a regular check to see that all remains safe throughout the activity.

To get around this problem you can place something between the rock and the ropes so that it is protected. The most effective padding to use is a piece of hard-wearing carpet which, if you tie cord through the ends, can be secured in place by attaching it to the anchor.

Regardless of how many anchor points you select they should all be connected together to come to one central point. This is most easily achieved by using a length of rope to construct the whole anchor. It is advisable to use a non-stretch rope for this. A climbing rope has lots of stretch in it – this is necessary to help it absorb shock in a fall. If used to connect a number of anchors together it will create an anchor point that has a certain amount of stretch in it. This stretch will be accentuated when a climber's weight comes on to the climbing rope and the attachment point at the edge of the crag will rub up and down the rock. This chaffing of the rope will cause considerable wear and tear and may, in an extreme case, cut through the rope.

By using a non-stretch rope this problem is largely eliminated. Furthermore, this type of rope is much more hard-wearing. It is worth making the point here that non-stretch ropes should not be used as climbing rope, as they do not have the same elasticity as climbing ropes. The shock loading on the anchors and belay system is considerably greater in the event of a fall and might result in bodily injury or anchor failure.

The only exception to this is perhaps on the sandstone outcrops of southern England where climbs are very short and considerable erosion is caused by ropes seesawing back and forth over the edge of the outcrop. Also, the rock is so abrasive that ordinary climbing ropes wear out very quickly indeed.

There are a number of ways to bring multiple anchors to one central point. Photo 1 illustrates a suitable method. The all important factor to remember whichever method you use is that if one should fail there must be no shock loading on the remaining anchors.

Obviously, the more anchors you have, the more rope you will need to connect them. It may be possible to connect two anchors together with a sling to create one attachment point in which case you will save on rope. Photos 2 and 3 show different methods of using a sling to bring two anchors to one point. (See vol. one for other suggestions.)

Getting the tension to each anchor can be a bit problematical. One way to make it easier is to tie the end of the rope into the first anchor. Having done that, clip a large karabiner into the abseil loop on your harness and clip the rope into it. Take the rope to the next anchor and clip it in. Now clip back through the krab on your abseil loop and take the rope to the next anchor. Keep going like this until you have clipped all the anchors. Using tension off the criss cross of ropes that you have, move to the position in which you want the anchor ropes to be. You'll need to feed them all through the krab on your abseil loop as you move. Once you are satisfied that they are all under tension and in position, make some final adjustments, take the whole bunch of ropes out of the krab on your harness and tie them all in a great big overhand knot. Photo 4 shows a simplified version.

To be certain that the tension remains equal throughout, you

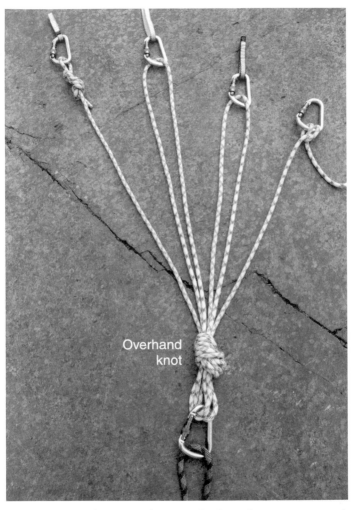

Overhand
knot

1 Using the rope to bring multiple anchors to one central
point.

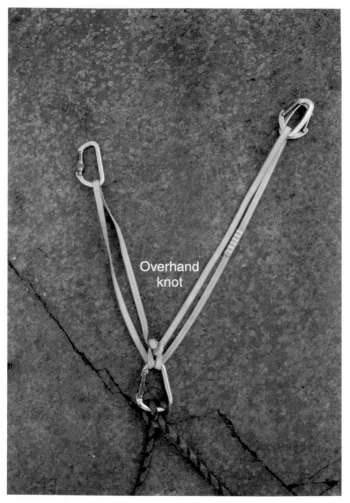

Overhand
knot

2 Two anchors brought to one point using a sling with an
overhand knot in the middle.

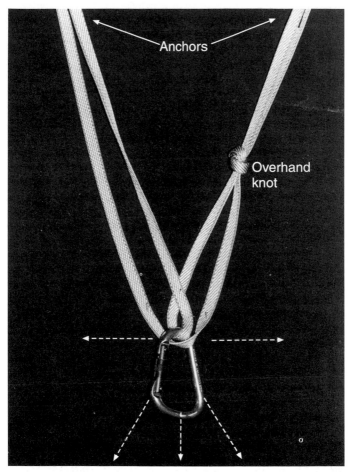

3 Two anchors brought to one point, allowing for sideways movement but retaining equal load on both. Tie an overhand in both sides to reduce shock loading if one should fail.

can return to each anchor point and secure the rope with a clove hitch – though it is not at all important to do this.

The loops formed by the large overhand knot may be too bulky to accommodate a karabiner safely. If this is the case, divide the ropes equally between a couple of screwgate krabs.

This will be your attachment point for the climbing rope. The karabiner or karabiners that you use here will be subjected to considerable wear and tear against the rock. Ideally, use steel screwgates or, as previously suggested, use a piece of carpet to stop them rubbing directly on the rock.

Clip the karabiners in so that the gates face uppermost and the opening end points down the crag. Sometimes karabiner screwgates can rattle themselves undone, but if you place them this way they are much less likely to do so. Another method of attaching the climbing rope to the anchor uses a large figure eight descendeur (photo 5). This method has clear safety advantages in that there is no possibility of a karabiner undoing itself or one of your students unclipping accidentally. Unfortunately, the rope runs against the rock during taking in and lowering creating a more serious abrasive action, as well as more friction. Using this method it is important to place carpet protection between the rope and rock. It is a particularly suitable method to use if the anchor point hangs freely over the edge of the crag.

If you don't have a spare rope available for rigging anchors together to one central point you will have to use slings. Be very careful to ensure that the tension is equally divided amongst the anchor points. It would appear to be a straight-forward task but it is usually not so easy to achieve as satisfactory a result as is possible with a separate rope. If you have to connect slings together because they are not long enough, you will need to use screwgate krabs at each connection. Some people lark's-foot slings together to create extra length but this is not as safe or reliable as using karabiners.

If you need to shorten slings it is possible to do so by tying

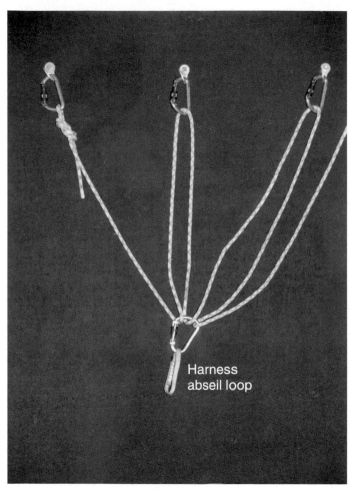

Harness
abseil loop

4 An effective system to get multiple anchors under equal tension.

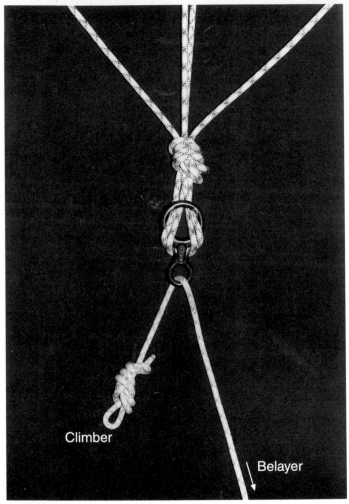

Climber

Belayer

5 Figure eight descendeur used in place of screwgate karabiner at anchor point. Note that ropes will rub against the rock unless anchor point is hanging free.

an overhand or figure eight knot to achieve the desired length.

Occasionally, the anchors may not be situated in the most desirable line for the anticipated loading. In such cases it is possible to place a directional anchor, preferably anchors, to hold the attachment point in position. Whilst these anchors will not bear the brunt of the force or load, they should nonetheless be as solid as the main anchors. A sideways pull can generate a fair amount of force and, of course, if the anchors come out unexpectedly under the load, the climber may swing and sustain an injury. Photo 6 shows a suggestion for retaining directional stability.

*Personal safety whilst rigging anchors or working close to the edge of a crag is paramount. You should always ensure that you are tied into an anchor of some description even if it has to be on a long cow's tail to permit free movement across the top of the crag. At assessment, personal safety is an important aspect of overall performance.*

## TOP ROPING

To set up an anchor for belaying from the top of the crag you must observe one or two important principles of safety.

Firstly, you should arrange your position so that you can see the climb in its entirety and secondly you must be directly above the climber you are belaying. This ideal is not always achievable and some situations may necessitate dropping down to a ledge below the edge of the crag. If you are not able to position yourself so that anyone you bring up the climb can move off easily to safe ground before untying from the rope, you might have to consider lowering them back down to the ground.

It is well worth considering belaying climbers with a direct belay. This method has a number of advantages over the more traditional method of belaying off your harness. It means that you are not committed to take the full weight of the climber if

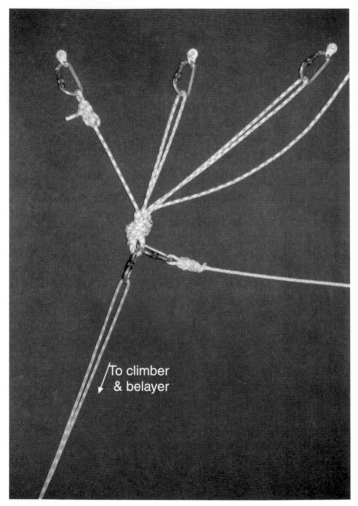

6 Side tension anchor for stabilising main anchor.

he or she falls off. Neither will you have to 'escape from the system' if a problem occurs. It goes without saying that your anchor points should be one hundred per cent solid for a direct belay, as the load will be transmitted directly to the anchors. A similar anchor set-up at the top of the crag to that used for arranging a bottom rope is therefore quite sensible. For comfort, safety and ease of operation the attachment point for the belaying method ought to be slightly above you and well back from the edge of the crag. This precludes the use of a belay plate because you need to operate such a device from behind. Normally you would use an Italian hitch or a descendeur, both of which can be safely operated from below.

When using a direct belaying method in this way you must take care of your own personal safety by clipping yourself in to the anchor point as well. This should be done separately by means of a sling or 'cow's tail'. Snake slings, which have a number of sections separated by bar-tack stitching, are particularly useful for this, as you can adjust your position very easily when needed. Photo 7 shows a suggested set-up clearly.

If you choose to belay climbers from within the system you do so in a normal climbing way, but bear in mind the fact that your ability to move around is severely restricted.

## BELAYING METHODS FROM BELOW

As stated earlier, bottom roping systems are infinitely preferable because they involve more people. With only a short demonstration and explanation of important safety considerations you can let the group belay each other – provided that you are on hand to oversee the whole operation.

Arranging the rope through an anchor point at the top of the climb will generate a certain amount of friction that helps the belayers hold the rope. In this situation any loading of the rope will create an upward-pulling force on the belayers and this should be taken into account. If you have light people belaying heavier climbers you may need to arrange an anchor that will prevent them being pulled up the cliff if the climber falls off. Such anchors may not always be found easily, in which case you might decide to use other participants to add extra weight to the belayer. They can be clipped together with slings from the front of the harness into the back of the harness of the person in front of them.

If suitable upward-pulling anchors are readily available the belayer only need be clipped in. Arrange the attachment so that any load generated by holding a climber is transmitted fairly directly through the belayer and on to the anchor.

Belayers should be positioned close in to the crag to avoid the possibility that a load might drag them in towards the bottom of the cliff. If the nature of the terrain dictates that you have to belay away from the bottom of the crag it is essential to tie the belayer into an upward-pulling anchor.

There are a number of ways to utilise as many people as possible in the belaying. One person should be attached to the belay device and be the main operator. Another can stand at the bottom of the crag facing out and pull down on the rope as the climber moves up. The belayer takes the rope through the belay device and there should always be another person acting as safety back-up on the dead or controlling rope.

The type of belay device or system that you use is entirely one of personal choice. The Gri Gri is a very good device for novices to use as it will lock even if everyone lets go. Some climbers, with long experience, find the device a little awkward to use at first and the temptation is to dismiss it out of hand. If you are teaching people who have never used any other device to use the Gri Gri, you will find that most will pick up the basic principles quite quickly. The Italian hitch is also a good method, as is any modern belay device. Be wary of using older style Sticht plates, as they have a tendency to jam up at the least convenient moment. See Chapter 8 on Belaying (page 348) for ways to operate these devices.

When instructing the use of a belay system, teach a method that is fairly simple to understand. The most important aspect is that the belayers must not let go of the dead rope or controlling rope. You can work out your own methodology for this – many people have their own particular way to do things. Brief everyone on what is to happen during the climb; as soon as the climber reaches the end of the climb; and whilst the climber is being lowered back to the ground. Before any lowering can take place the climber should place all of his or her weight on the rope. The belayers lock off the rope whilst the climber does this. Once you are satisfied that all the weight is on the rope the belayers can begin lowering very slowly. Do not allow any rope to run suddenly through the device. If you do let rope run quickly the climber may experience the feeling that the rope has been let go and will try to grab hold of the rock taking their weight off the rope. The lowering should only be speeded up once the climber has got used to the sensation of being lowered with someone else in control of their destiny.

Whatever system you choose to use it is vitally important that you remain in a position where you can control and supervise everyone involved, continually emphasising the importance of safety.

## DEALING WITH PROBLEMS

Few problems are likely to occur that are not solved easily and simply. Probably the most common occurrence of all is that of 'stuck' climber. This happens mainly through fear or lack of experience to see what can and cannot be used as a handhold or foothold. Sometimes it occurs through outright fear and the climber becomes 'frozen' to the rock face. In both cases a solution may be simply to talk the climber through a sequence of moves or to encourage with sympathetic words. If, on the other hand, the climber has managed somehow to get a foot or a knee jammed in a crack you will almost certainly have to go to their assistance. One of the more unusual incidents I have experienced was a solidly jammed helmet!

Anyone who is stuck or refuses to move and will not take their weight on the rope to be lowered back to the ground will require you to go to their assistance. This could be done by going around to the top of the crag and abseiling down by their side to talk them through the sequence or cajole them into being lowered. To do this will take quite a bit of time and take you away from your responsibilities to the rest of the group.

It is better to go to their assistance from below. One way to do this is as follows. Put a French prusik knot on to the live climbing rope just above the belayer and attach it to the abseil loop on your own harness. Move the prusik up the rope until you can lean out on it, putting tension on the rope in a counter balance situation. Having done this you can put a second prusik, such as a Klemheist, below the first and ascend the rope.

An alternative and very quick system is to attach a belay device below the first French prusik. If the rock is low angled you can simply walk up the rock taking in the rope through the belay device as you gain height. Make sure that the belayers give you some slack but don't ask them to take the rope out of the belay device completely. Photo 8 shows this set-up. Note that on easy angled rock the foot loop prusik may not even be necessary.

As you move up the French prusik will release itself but will act as an autobloc to prevent you slipping back down if you have to let go of the rope. Be careful though, French prusik knots do not always lock without a little assistance to start the process. Once you get to the stuck climber you can lean back on the prusik and ask the belayers to take the rope tight through the belay device and lock it off. This is by way of a back up. You are now in a position to talk the stuck climber through the moves and being by the side of them may be sufficient moral encouragement to do this. As they move up

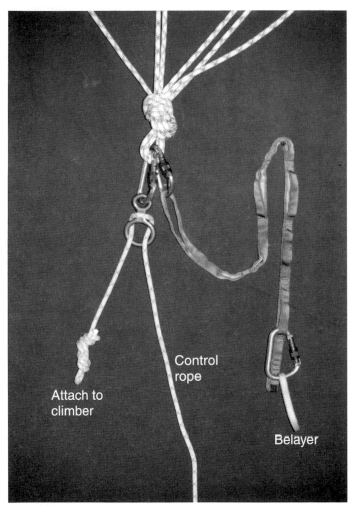

7 Top roping set-up.

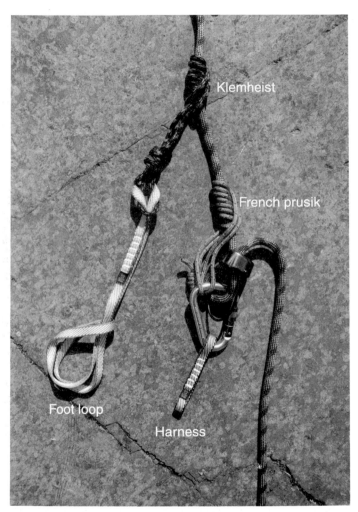

8 Ascending set-up to rescue 'stuck' climber.

9 Bottom roping. The anchor point has been arranged over the edge to reduce erosion.

10 Bottom roping. It is easier to supervise two groups when climbs are close together.

you can continue to ascend alongside, taking in the rope through the belay device as you move up, using your weight against theirs as a counter balance. If this fails and they do not want to climb on or be lowered down alone, you can clip into their harness tie on loop or the abseil loop and go down with them in an accompanied abseil. All you need to do is simply connect yourself to the tie on loop of their harness – a quick draw will do – and abseil down to the ground with them. Don't forget to ask the belayer to take the rope out of their belay device before you begin to descend.

All the time that you are doing this you will still of course be responsible for ensuring the safety of any other ropes that you may have set up, but at least you will never be out of sight of what is going on. Of course, if something major were to go awry on another climb it would take you some time to get there to render assistance. If you are on your own supervising the group it may be preferable to call a temporary halt to the other climb whilst you sort out the problem in hand.

If by some unlucky coincidence a climber is injured whilst on the route, the same method can be used to go to their assistance and descend to the ground under your control.

This is by far the simplest way to deal with a stuck climber. There are some others. For example, if you are using a Gri Gri, there is no need for a prusik. You could take over the belayer's Gri Gri by clipping yourself into the karabiner that attaches it to their harness and unclipping them from it. You can ascend the rope pulling the slack through the Gri Gri as you ascend and you can, with practice, use the Gri Gri as an abseiling device.

Keep it simple! is the key to solving these sorts of problems, for simplicity often means speed and efficiency.

# 3 Abseiling with Groups

Abseiling is perceived by many to be a fun activity and may in some cases be set up entirely divorced from the sport of rock climbing to which it rightly belongs.

In itself there is nothing wrong with this philosophy but there are wider implications if it is used by non-climbers who do not understand the technical aspects of rock climbing ropework.

There are a number of important considerations to bear in mind when choosing a suitable venue. Of greatest significance is accessibility. The group will be much easier to control if you are able to arrange for them to wait well back from the edge of the crag but when they need to come forward to take their turn they are not exposed to the risk of falling over the cliff edge as they approach and before being attached to a safety rope.

Take time to consider the situation at the bottom of the crag too. Ideally this should be fairly flat and free of danger. If you don't have anyone to supervise the group at the bottom of the crag you will need to position them in a place where you are able to keep an eye on them. It is also important to move them away from the foot of the abseil out of line of fire of anything that might accidentally be knocked down the crag.

You may decide that you want people to return to the top of the crag after they have disconnected from the rope. To this end, try to choose a venue that has an easy and obvious walking route back to the top.

For people, young or older, who have never abseiled before choose a crag that is not too steep. Vertical and overhanging crags are intimidating places for those not familiar with a crag environment and people may become preoccupied with their fear rather than concentrating on and being able to savour the experience. Neither should the crag be too high, about 10–15 m (35–50 ft) is ideal. This height means that you will be able to get people down an abseil many times. The more they do, the more confident they will become and you can move on to more exciting things more quickly.

## SAFETY

First experiences of abseiling necessitate the use of a safety rope. This is not only a sensible precaution but is also a great confidence booster. The safety rope should either be tied in directly to the harness as per the manufacturer's recommendation or clipped in to the abseil loop of the harness with a screwgate karabiner. Normally, this would be attached to the loop below the abseil device. Photo 11 shows the basic set-up.

It is also advisable to set up the abseil rope so that it can be released under load. More problems arise in group abseiling situations than they do in 'normal' abseiling by experienced climbers when it is used as a means of descent.

The main problems that occur include clothing stuck in the abseil device or, much worse, hair, which can be extremely painful. Paying close attention to these potential disasters prior to launching off will pay dividends and avoid the possibility that they might occur in the first instance. Another common occurrence is that the abseiler becomes so terrified that they are unable to complete the descent and, just as in climbing up, the abseiler may become 'frozen' to the rock face. Occasionally, someone might get their foot or leg jammed in a crack. In rare cases, the abseil device may become jammed or a knot appear in the rope.

If such problems do occur you will be well placed to deal with them if you set up a releasable abseil.

It is very simple to set up. Instead of securing the abseil rope with a figure eight knot directly to the anchor, connect it with an Italian hitch into an HMS karabiner clipped into the anchor. Tie off the Italian hitch securely with an appropriate method (see vol. one, page 21). If someone has a problem on the abseil

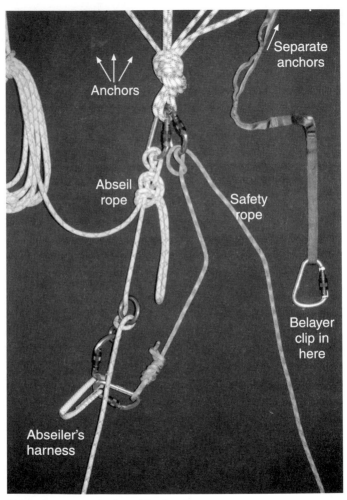

11 Basic set-up of releasable abseil.

you are then able to release the rope and take the strain on to the safety rope. This can be effected very quickly, a particularly important factor if someone gets their hair caught in a device when there is considerable urgency to act. Photo 12 shows the detail of the tied off Italian hitch in a realeasable abseil.

You should operate the safety rope as a direct belay and keep yourself out of the system. Obviously you must be tied in to the anchor but it is a good idea to allow yourself some room for manoeuvre and tie in with a long cow's tail. A snake sling is particularly useful for this (photo 11).

An Italian hitch is a good enough method with which to operate the safety rope. So also is a figure eight descendeur. Both of these belay methods allow you to stand in front of the anchor where you can be most useful. Belay devices have to be operated from behind and are therefore not so convenient.

## SIMPLE RESCUE SCENARIOS

By proper planning and setting up most problems are easily avoided. If something unforeseen does occur, it is preferable to solve it by working to the principle of 'simplest is quickest'. Do not get bogged down in overly complex solutions to problems.

For example, if an abseiler gets clothing stuck in an abseil device lock off the safety rope (as in photo 12 or in photo 57 vol. one) and then release the abseil rope until there is enough slack for them to pull the clothing out of the device. The safety rope can just be held tightly by hand without the need to tie it off, but you will have to work quickly. If you want to ensure there is a safety back up you could put a French prusik on the loaded safety rope and attach it to the anchor or tie off the device you are using to safeguard them with. (Provided you don't have to move too far away from the anchor, you could always have a French prusik safety back up on the safety rope for those just-in-case situations.)

Once the victim has released the clothing from the device

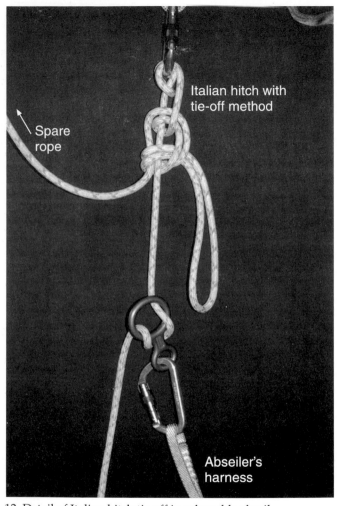

Italian hitch with
tie-off method

Spare
rope

Abseiler's
harness

12 Detail of Italian hitch tie off in releasable abseil.

you can take in the abseil rope tight, tie it off again, and continue with the abseil by lowering the victim's weight back on to the abseil rope, using the safety rope.

Hair caught in a device requires extremely quick action on your part and there may not be enough time to tie off the safety rope until you have released the abseil. Just so long as you have a tight hold on the safety and work with speed this has to be acceptable.

If someone is stuck, terrified and refusing to move any further, you should, to begin with, make every effort to talk them down. Words of comfort and encouragement are often the best solution to this type of problem. If words should meet with little success you might try taking over control of their descent yourself. This can be done by lowering both the safety and the abseil ropes simultaneously. You must ensure that the abseiler's full weight remains on one or both ropes at all times. If you allow slack to develop, the shock of falling back on to the rope before it becomes loaded may be too discouraging and frightening. It will be obvious here that you should ensure there is sufficient abseil rope available to achieve this, though of course you could always allow the abseil rope to fall to the ground, as there will always be sufficient length of safety rope.

If someone is so terrified that even this solution proves unworkable, or they have a foot stuck in a crack, the best option is to go down and help them abseil. A suggested way to do this safely is as follows.

Take all the load on to the safety rope and secure it by tying it off. Release enough of the abseil rope so that you can attach yourself and then tie it off again. Connect yourself to the abseil rope using a long sling shortened to make one long attachment and one short. Make sure that you include a safety back up French prusik attached to your leg loop. Then release yourself from the cow's tail attachment to the anchor. Abseil down to the victim and disconnect them from their abseil device. Remove it from the rope.

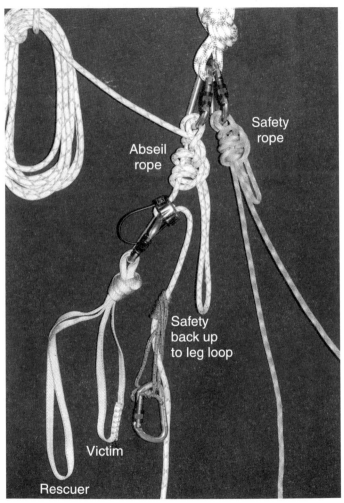

13 Rescue set-up for 'stuck' abseiler.

Next, connect the abseil loop of their harness on to the short loop from your own abseil rig. When you do this, try to lift the victim up a little, so that the safety rope connection goes slack. If you think they are able, you could ask them to pull themselves up on one of the ropes. Once you have the victim secured to your abseil device you can unclip them from the safety rope. Abseil down together to the ground (Photo 13).

An alternative to the method suggested would be to use an entirely separate rope for your own abseil. You may decide to set one up ready 'just in case'. The method of rescue is identical to that previously described.

By far the most important factor is that you must not become involved in unnecessary and overly complex solutions.

# 4 MIA

*Improvised Rescue*

Many of the techniques required for the MIA, particularly improvised rescue, are covered in vol. one. There are, however, one or two other aspects not dealt with there and others where there have been additional techniques or improvements made to existing ones.

## IMPROVISED RESCUE

A great deal of emphasis is placed on the ability to conduct rescues from crags using only normal climbing equipment. Placing such importance on these skills not only allows the instructor to operate with confidence in the knowledge that they possess but it also presents an opportunity to hone rope techniques and develop a greater understanding of the principles of good stance organisation, selection of anchors and avoidance of basic problems.

It is important to recognise from the outset that the simplest solution to a problem is very often the most efficient and that to embark on complex and long-winded fanciful rope manoeuvres may not be the most appropriate way to solve a problem.

For example, a client or student who is having difficulty on a section of a climb may need some help getting over the hard bit. To effect this the instructor might rig a simple assisted hoist. If the instructor, however, feels strong enough to do it, they may just simply pull the client hand over hand. Obviously, the rope needs to be taken in through the belay device so that security at all times is assured, but there is absolutely nothing wrong with this solution.

Another example might be in the case of forced evacuation

from the crag. If you are able to get down to the ground in one abseil or lower, even if it means tying two ropes together, it is preferable to fix the rope in place, retreat and recover your equipment at a later stage. Obviously, if you are likely to need your gear further down the mountain or you are in a remote spot, you will need to retrieve as much of it as possible on the way down.

## SOLVING SIMPLE PROBLEMS

At assessment you will normally be asked to solve a number of simple and common problems in addition to at least one major scenario. Simple problems include the following:

### A knot in the rope

If, despite all your careful preparations, you discover an overhand knot in the climbing rope between you and your client, either while leading a pitch or while taking in the rope, it will be necessary to either undo it or, more straightforward, move it down the rope. If your client has a rope attached to a second client the best thing to do is to ask them to move the knot down the rope until it reaches their tie on knot. Once the client reaches your stance you can then untie the knot by first clipping them into the belay anchor with a sling and releasing them from the end of the rope. Untie the offending knot and then tie back on to the end of the rope.

A client who is tied on to the end of the rope with no second rope attached can undo the mysterious knot by simply moving it down towards their tie on and then making a large loop to step through in order to undo the offending knot.

In no circumstances should you ask them to untie from the end of the rope whilst you are out of reach and without the ability to check one hundred per cent that they have retied on to the rope end correctly.

## Stuck runner

If a client is unable to retrieve a runner from its placement it may be better for you to descend and take the runner out yourself. First of all you should try talking the client through a procedure which you work out from your recall of how the runner was placed. If this fails, the client may well reach a point where the problem is made worse and the runner is beyond retrieval. You may, of course, decide that you are content to leave it behind and carry on with the climb.

If you decide that you will get the runner back yourself, solving the problem is largely one of good organisation. Bring your client or clients up to the stance and secure them to the belay. You may find it quicker to climb back down to the runner to retrieve it. You can ask one of your clients to belay you as you do so and to safeguard you as you climb back up.

You might prefer to arrange your ropes in such a way as you can abseil down to the stuck gear. What you might choose to do is to abseil on the rope between your first and second client and ask the first to belay you on your own rope whilst you descend. Always abseil down with a French prusik back up, as this will allow you to release both hands to retrieve the runner. You can then climb back up the route and your client can take in the rope as you do so.

Another solution is to abseil down and to prusik back up to the stance. You would normally do this on your own rope, without necessarily untying from the end. Simply drop a loop of rope down the crag, enough to reach a little over halfway to the runner and then fix the rope to the anchor. Attach your abseil device to the fixed rope and descend on this. As you go down, the rope attached to your harness will give you the extra distance required to reach the stuck runner.

It is important to work methodically in arranging ropes to descend otherwise you might become horrendously entangled and spend unnecessary time sorting out the mess you have created.

## Client climbs past a runner

This is a favourite problem offered by assessors, but in truth it should rarely occur! Arranging your stance so that you have a view of the whole pitch and good communication will prevent this happening. Unfortunately, despite your best efforts, it is inevitable that it will happen occasionally. Clients frequently become so absorbed and focused on the task in hand that they pay little attention to anything other than making the moves. Any time that a client asks for slack rope you should question why they need it. Normally it will be to climb down a little bit but if they say that they need it to climb past a runner then clearly something is amiss. If you are aware of the problem you can prevent them climbing more than a foot or so above the runner and can easily ask them to climb back down until level with the runner. If, however, they climb a good few feet above the problem is altogether more serious and will require prompt action on your part.

If a client were to fall off a few feet above a runner the fall could be quite long and in doing so they might sustain an injury. As soon as you realise there is something amiss you need to ask them to stay exactly where they are whilst you arrange for a loop of rope to be sent down to them. The best thing to do is to tie off the belay device and, using the slack rope from where you are tied in to the anchor, drop a loop down to them. This loop should have a knot and a karabiner in it which the client will clip into the abseil loop of their harness. You attach the rope to the anchor via an Italian hitch and ask them to take their weight on the rope. Lower them back down until level with the runner and regain control of the climbing rope through the belay device. Once they are secured again you can ask them to untie the loop, remove the runner and climb on.

If the client can get into a reasonably comfortable position and can reach the rope that goes between you, the instructor, and the runner below the client, it may be possible for them to pull through a bit of slack rope, tie a figure eight or overhand knot in the rope and clip it in to a screwgate on the harness. Obviously the client must be very comfortable and able to use both hands to tie the knot.

## Cannot climb a difficult section of the route

If you are part way up a climb and one of your clients finds it too difficult to do the moves you can assist them by keeping the rope very tight. More often than not you'll be able to help them over the hard bit with assistance from the rope. If this fails, you may have to arrange an assisted hoist. This can be effected without the need to escape from the system. Tie off the belay device and put a French prusik autobloc on the live rope. Drop a loop of the dead rope down to the client with a krab clipped in. This krab is then attached to the client's abseil loop on their harness or just into the tie in loop. Undo the tied off belay device and tension all the ropes. If the client pulls on the only rope that travels downwards and you pull on the spare rope at the same time you will both be able to effect the hoist. See photo 69 in vol. one.

Once the difficult section has been overcome, the client can release the loop of rope and you can regain control through the belay device. If you leave the French prusik on whilst you are sorting out the ropes the client will be safeguarded throughout.

This method of hoisting can only really work if you have enough rope available to implement it. If your client is more than a third of the rope's length below the stance you will need to consider the addition of a sling or slings, connected on to the end of the loop that is dropped to them. If you have enough slings, you could add a considerable length to the loop. Each sling should ideally be connected to another via a screwgate karabiner, though if none is available, lark's-footing slings together may be the best alternative.

Should the client be a long way below or off to one side, where it is impossible to throw them a loop, you may need to effect a hoist from within the system. This is set up in exactly the same way as the hoist shown in vol. one photo 71 where the anchor is replaced by your belay device. This method is obviously laborious and time-consuming and as soon as the client is within reach you should revert to an assisted hoist.

## Client fails to follow a pitch

If, despite your best efforts, a client cannot follow a pitch and there is harder climbing further up the route, you might decide it is better to retreat. To do this you will need to lower the client back down to the previous stance and secure them there whilst you arrange to retreat.

If the anchor point on the previous stance was a complex one you may not be able to trust the client to re-rig it. In this case you will probably choose to arrange a counter balance abseil.

Lower the client back to the stance and ask them to stand or sit securely on the ledge. Escape from the system and make sure that the rope to the client is backed up with a tied off Italian hitch to the anchor and leave the French prusik in place. Decide what anchor you are going to use to retreat from. If you have nothing else available this may have to be the anchors that you are tied into. It is preferable, of course, to leave behind the minimum amount of gear so alternatives should be arranged if possible.

It is likely that you will need to leave, at the very least, a sling and krab behind so that the abseil rope can be retrieved easily. Once you have arranged the abseil anchor thread the rope through it and keep pulling it through until it is tight to your client down below. For the moment leave the tied off Italian hitch and French prusik in place. Attach yourself to the rope on the opposite side to the client's rope and make sure that you put on a French prusik back up to the leg loop.

Retrieve all the gear you are not leaving behind, position yourself as closely as possible to the anchor and then untie the Italian hitch back up, clearing any other gear remaining. Pull through any slack rope until you are tight on the rope and heave backwards with all your might! As you heave back you must hold your abseil rope tightly in one hand whilst you release the original French prusik securing the client. Once that is released and recovered you can abseil down to join your client, arrange a suitable anchor for both of you and then retrieve the ropes to continue abseiling down.

If you do not have enough rope to reach the client in one abseil, which will be the case if the pitch was longer than half of the rope length, you will need to abseil down as far as is necessary to create sufficient rope to reach their stance and arrange another abseil anchor to continue your descent to the client.

Photos 14, 15 and 16 show a suggested set-up for the counter balance abseil descent as described. Always remember to tie a knot in the loose end of the rope that you are abseiling on.

Of course, if you are able to lower your client to the ground in one rope length, or even by joining two ropes together, you should do so, for it will be easier to retreat yourself, even if you have to make the descent yourself in two stages. Photo 61 on page 137 of vol. one shows a way to pass a knot through a lowering device using a French prusik. Turn the page upside down for improved clarity!

Other simple problems may be presented to you, but the ability to cope with these described should equip you with the basic knowledge to solve most of them simply and efficiently.

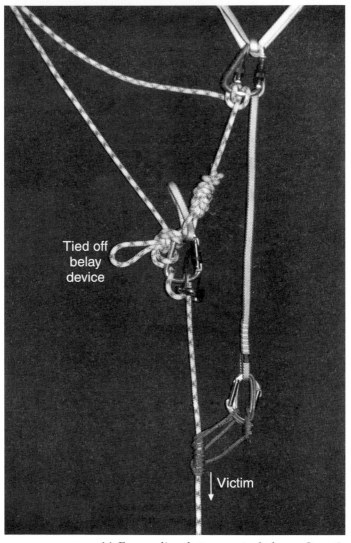

14 Escape directly to counter balance: Stage 1.

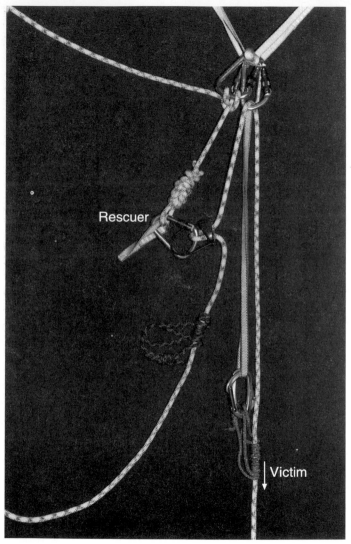

15 Escape directly to counter balance: Stage 2.

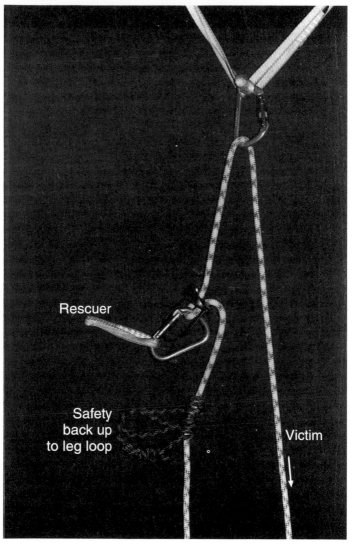

16 Escape directly to counter balance: Stage 3.

## COMPLEX SCENARIOS

At assessment you will be given at least one complex rescue problem to solve. The nature of the problem will depend on the type of ground you are climbing on and will generally be something fairly realistic. Assessors have differing ways of presenting and creating these scenarios and it is important for you, as the candidate, to be sure that you understand fully what has been presented. There is a temptation to try to outguess the assessor and assume that the scene has been set for you to demonstrate a particular technique or set piece. You would be well advised to concentrate on solving the problem as you see it at the time it is presented and to do so in as efficient a way as is possible.

By breaking down the procedure into different elements to arrive at a satisfactory result, you will be able to concentrate your efforts to greater effect.

Every scenario will be different, depending on the nature of the climb and, though it is possible to follow basic procedures, you will invariably have to cope with idiosyncrasies. The real skill of the instructor in these situations is tested to its maximum.

A selection of scenarios follows. These are not exhaustive by any means but should serve to equip you with the necessary skills and procedural elements to manage other possible problems.


### Unconscious and injured client

The priority with any unconscious victim is to get down to them as quickly as possible. Ideally this should be accomplished in a few minutes, 3–4 being a reasonable time to aim for. Anything that takes longer than this might be deemed to be inefficient and dangerous. To achieve this ideal requires considerable practice and the ability to work totally unflustered and virtually flawlessly.

Priority must be given to whatever is the quickest method of escaping the system and descending to the injured climber. If your anchor set-up is simple and you are within arm's reach of the anchor, it is often just as quick to go straight into a counter balance abseil as you escape. Having an unconscious victim means that you are most likely to have to descend anyway so, if it is straightforward to rig the counter balance, it is advisable to do so.

Note that the set-up is very similar to that previously described in the simple rescue scenario *Client fails to follow a pitch*, illustrated in photos 14, 15 and 16, which show the set-up for escaping directly into the counter balance descent. By working quickly, given that everything is in your favour, it is possible to complete the procedure within the few minutes' limit.

If, on the other hand, you are a long way away from your anchor, or you have a complex anchor set-up, it is probably more efficient in terms of time to escape the system and abseil down to the victim. Having made your casualty comfortable and satisfied yourself that they can be left, you will then need to return to the stance to set up a retreat which can, once again, be a counter balance abseil.

Never discount the possibility that even an unconscious person might be lowered to a ledge where not only will they be more comfortable but also make your task considerably easier.

It cannot be stressed too highly that speed is of the utmost importance in order to get the casualty into a position where they are able to breathe comfortably and, hopefully, regain consciousness.

For methods of escaping the system refer to vol. one page 144. Instead of backing up the French prusik with a figure eight knot directly back to the anchor, it is preferable to tie it back with an Italian hitch, tied off. This will enable you to convert quickly to a lower and will not present you with problems if the French prusik slips and the rope becomes tight on the safety back up.

The same system can be set up to go to the aid of an injured second who is hurt, but still conscious. Though speed is obviously important, it is not as vital as in the case of an unconscious victim.

### Client falls off on a traverse and is unable to regain contact with the rock

This is a good one to be given! It will test your abilities to their max. It is an unenviable situation to find yourself in but, mercifully, a very rare one indeed. Take, for example, the following scenario. A climb has a 5 m (15 ft) traverse above an overhang. The leader should try to arrange the stance as close to the end of the traverse as possible and slightly above the finish of the traverse. Ideally, the belay should be taken directly above the middle of the traverse if it is a short one, or slightly off centre towards the end, if it is a longer one. This cannot always be achieved.

Photo 17 shows a traverse situation in less than ideal circumstances. Let us suppose that the moment the second unclips the runner above his head, he falls off. Clearly he will fall into unclimbable ground.

A solution to the problem is suggested as follows:

The leader must first secure the rope by tying off the belay device and putting on a French prusik which is fixed to the central belay loop on the harness tie in.

Don't remove the belay device.

Next, the leader should take up some coils of slack from his own end of the rope and attempt to throw a loop to the fallen climber. Having successfully achieved this, the fallen climber will connect the loop to their harness tie on point, preferably with a screwgate krab. As can be seen in the photo 18, one end of this loop is already fixed and the other should be attached to

17 A traverse problem.

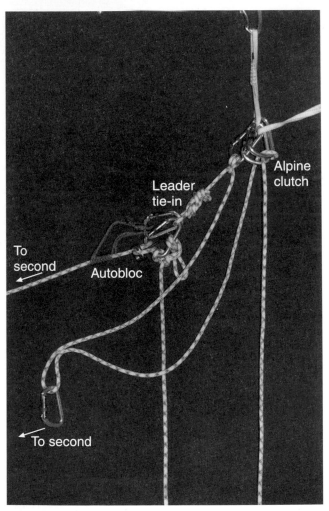

18 Rescuing a second who has fallen off a traverse.

the anchor with an Italian hitch, or preferably an Alpine clutch (see vol. one, page 53).

The procedure now requires considerable dexterity on the part of the leader and great strength on the part of the second. As the second pulls on the fixed rope the leader must take in through the Alpine clutch and pay out through the belay device. (Don't forget to release it first!) By this combination you should be able to swing the second across until he or she is directly below the stance. From here you can hoist them directly up to the belay, using a direct one to one assisted hoist. If your client can regain contact with the rock he or she should climb up and you can take in through the Alpine clutch.

It is an extraordinarily difficult manoeuvre to effect. It is made considerably easier if the second is able to maintain contact with the rock but if they are hanging in space over the lip of an overhang it can be quite problematical. There will be considerable friction and you must not disregard the possibility that the rope may be damaged or, at worst, cut by running along the lip of the overhang.

Once you are both on the stance, secure the second to the anchor, untie them from the end of the rope and pull it through the runners on the traverse before tying them back on to the end and continuing. You will, of course, have to decide whether or not to retrieve the runners. If you do decide to get them back it is easier to ask the client to belay you whilst you reverse the climb, retrieve them and then climb back up to the stance and continue with the ascent.

If, in the very worst case, your second is injured and unable to help, or you can't throw the rope to them, you will need to escape and deliver it yourself or get into a position where you are able to drop a loop.

Be extremely careful doing this. You cannot simply escape the system utilising the anchors above your head. If you do, when you remove the belay device from the live rope to transfer the load to the anchor there will be a straightening out of the tensioned ropes which is accompanied by a sudden shock loading and a certain amount of slack rope.

It is better to re-arrange the anchor so that the loaded point remains in the same position as if you were still belaying the second. To do this you will need to arrange an upward pulling anchor from below and behind you which is connected to the main upper anchors and adjusted so that the load remains in an identical position to that when you were belaying from within the system. Having rigged this complex arrangement, you must then move out along the traverse on the tensioned rope, either hanging from it or by climbing along attached with a cow's tail, to a position where you can drop a loop of spare rope.

If the client is injured you may need to prusik down the rope to them to attach the loop yourself.

Needless to say, this technique requires a good deal of practice!

**You have set up a stacked abseil and a client gets clothing caught in the device and is unable to descend – client is unable to touch the rock**

Another interesting problem to solve! (Turn to page 67 for stacked abseils.)

The first thing to do is to secure the abseiler so that they cannot move any further down the rope. If you safeguard stacked abseils as suggested later, you will already have the belay device on the rope and can lean back on it to create the necessary tension. Lock off the belay device and put a French prusik on both ropes above the belay device. This should be connected by a short quick draw to your abseil loop.

Put on a second prusik loop above the French prusik to use as a foot loop. You can now prusik up the rope to the stuck abseiler. All the time that you do this the rope will remain under tension, preventing the person from sliding any further down the rope. Photo 8 shows this set-up, though on a single rope.

As you stand up in the foot loop, take in the rope through the belay device and make sure you pull it as tight as possible. As you sit back, the tension should come on to the French prusik which will support your weight while you move the foot loop up to gain more height.

On arrival at the victim make sure that you get as close as possible and maintain your weight on the rope. Try to release whatever has got caught in the abseil device but if it proves a problem do not waste time – cut it with a sharp knife. Just make sure that you cut away from any ropes!

You can now do one of two things. Abseil back down (having first removed the foot prusik but not the French prusik) and, once on the ground, ask the victim to continue abseiling. Or connect yourself to the victim's abseil device with a spare sling or quick draw and then remove your own belay device from the rope. You can then abseil down together with you controlling the descent through the French prusik that remains attached to your harness.

If the client can touch the rock and, maybe, stand on a small ledge or foothold, it may be possible for them to release the offending object themselves and then gradually get their weight back on to the abseil. You must make sure that you keep the rope taut throughout this exercise, otherwise there may be a shock loading on the rope when the client puts their weight back on to the abseil.

You must never ask them to unclip from the abseil device in any circumstances.

## You are at the top of a multi-pitch climb and the client cannot finish the route due to an injury

This presents a dilemma. Do you decide to retreat down the crag or spend a bit of time hoisting the client to the top of the crag from where you can easily walk off?

Hoisting presents its own particular problems. Not least, it can be extremely difficult to effect and to operate efficiently. Vol. one contains all you are likely to need with regard to hoisting. Photos 19 and 20 illustrate two other efficient methods of hoisting that might also be considered. Both of these have the advantage that they can be operated from within the system.

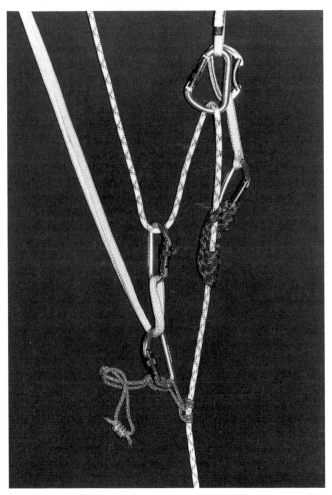

19 5:1 pulley hoist that can be executed from within the system.

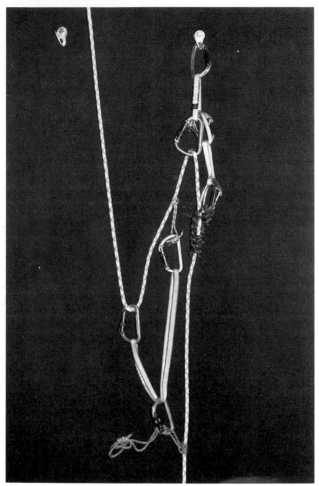

20 7:1 pulley hoist that can be executed from within the system.

# 5 MIA

*Abseiling, stance organisation, multi-pitch climbing and teaching lead climbing*

NOTE: *in this chapter the techniques described assume that you will be climbing with two students or clients.*

## STACKED ABSEILS

If you need to abseil off a climb with clients the safest and most effective method is to use a technique known as the stacked abseil. This technique requires you to go down first, leaving your client or clients set up on the abseil before you descend. As with all rope techniques it is important to be well organised and methodical in your approach.

On arrival at the top of the climb arrange your anchor in the normal manner. When you bring up each of your clients, get them to clip into the anchor using a long sling. This can be threaded through the harness tie on loops – the same ones through which you would thread the rope. The length of this cow's tail can be varied by tying a knot in the sling at the required length.

Once you have your clients secure in this way, arrange a similar set-up for yourself. Photo 21 shows a sling threaded through the correct parts of the harness and secured with a lark's foot.

Next you must arrange the ropes for the abseil. Be careful to ensure that, as you all untie from the ends, you do not drop any rope. A good safeguard is to attach one end of each rope to the anchor with a knot tied a little more than a metre from the end. This will usually leave you a long enough tail to loop around the abseil anchor and allow you to tie the ends of both ropes together. Obviously, if you think you need more, tie the

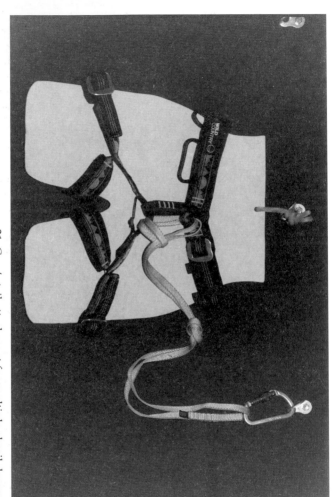

21 Cow's tail attachment for multiple abseil descents.

temporary fixing knot further along the rope. Once the ropes are securely in place you can then untie these temporary knots without fear of dropping the ropes down the crag accidentally.

Decide which order your clients will descend in and attach their belay devices to the abseil rope, one above the other. Normally you will need to attach each via a short extension – a quick draw is ideal for this. Make sure that you use screwgate krabs to attach both to the harness and to the abseil device. Attach clients one at a time, positioning them as comfortably as possible and allowing room for each to stand. As an extra security measure, and for practice in use, you can also arrange for each of them to have a French prusik safety back up attached to their leg loop. Whilst this offers a measure of security and is a good opportunity to practise abseiling with a safety back up you will invariably find that inexperienced students or clients will have great difficulty manipulating the back up and abseiling at the same time. It's a problem well worth consideration.

Place yourself on the abseil rope and make sure that you attach a French prusik safety back up to your harness leg loop. Once you are on the rope you can lean back with all your weight on the abseil rope and be held securely by the French prusik. Photo 22 shows the set up described. Ask each of your clients to undo their sling attachment and wrap the sling around their waist, clipping the krab back into it. By doing this you will have a ready-made cow's tail to clip them into the anchor after each stage of the abseil (photo 23). Unclip your own cow's tail and clear any gear that you are not leaving behind. Brief your clients well on the procedure to adopt for the descent, tell them that it is vitally important that they do not descend until instructed to do so.

Descend yourself to the next stance down (or to the ground if appropriate) from where you will do a second stage abseil. Arrange an anchor for yourself and your clients that is easy for them to clip into. Clip yourself in with the cow's tail. Make

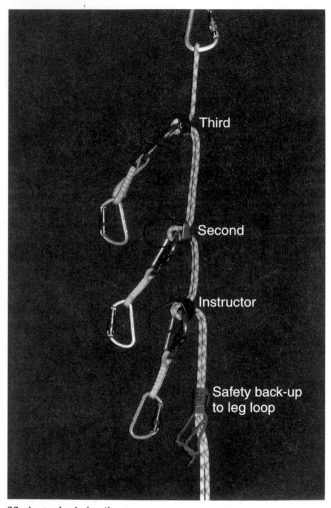

22 A stacked abseil set-up.

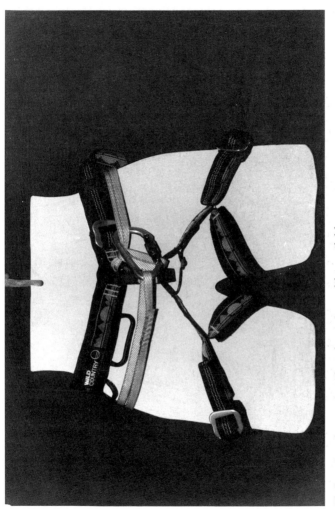

23 Stowing the cow's tail so that it is readily available.

sure that you keep some tension on the abseil rope throughout, as you are basically acting as the anchor person for your clients. By keeping the rope under tension you will prevent them from sliding down the rope.

This is best done by leaving yourself attached to the device you have used to abseil and leaving the French prusik safety back up in place. When you are ready call the first client down. On their arrival at the stance, take their cow's tail and clip it into the anchor. Keep tension on the abseil rope all the time. Once the first client is detached from the abseil you can then call the second one down. The same procedure of attaching to the anchor point applies.

When both clients are off the abseil you can detach yourself and retrieve the ropes. Set up the second stage and repeat the process.

It's worth pointing out here that with this method of stacked abseiling you need not necessarily descend to the next stance in one stage. If, for example, you think that you might go out of sight of your clients, or that you need to keep close by because they are nervous, you can actually descend in a number of stages without the need to rig intermediate stances. If you felt the need to, you could go down to a large ledge at, say, 20 m (65 ft) and then re-group there before continuing the descent.

Some people leave the clients clipped in at the top of the abseil with a cow's tail which has to be removed before they can descend. This is OK, provided you know that the clients will only undo the cow's tail and not something more important by mistake. It also requires your clients to let go of the abseil rope entirely to sort out gear. It is perhaps better to leave them attached only to the abseil rope via the abseil device and/or with a French prusik safety back up for those that have the experience to handle it.

This method of abseiling with clients is not suitable for anyone who has never abseiled before or who has very little experience of abseiling.

# MULTI-PITCH CLIMBING

Poor organisation and planning of stances and construction of belay anchors is one of the most frequently criticised aspects of an individual's skills observed during assessment. On the type of climbs appropriate at this level there is really very little excuse for shoddy belaying, as stances are normally fairly commodious and anchors plentiful.

All that is required is a little careful thought and, more importantly, planning. There are two different scenarios of stance organisation – that required for a guiding scenario, where the instructor will do all the belaying and that in which the clients or students will belay each other. The differences in actual methods of arranging anchors and organising the stance are much less clearly defined, but both require the same approach to safety and simplicity.

The main difference is that in the instructional scenario the emphasis will be on teaching students techniques that they are likely to need in order to go away and take care of themselves. Whilst guiding should always contain an element of instruction, for that will enhance the enjoyment of a day out, the emphasis should be placed on speedy and efficient movement, with as much climbing as can be reasonably achieved in a day.

There is a tendency amongst many instructors to over-instruct. An imbalance between action and words detracts somewhat from the whole ethos of the sport. Whilst we have an obligation to teach, if engaged to do so, we also have an obligation to give clients a good day out on the crags and to give them an opportunity to sample the true pleasures of rock climbing.

It is questionable whether anyone who is shown half a dozen or more differing ways of tying into anchors during a day out will retain the knowledge through to the next day, least of all in the time that elapses before they are able to go out on their own. It is perhaps better to concentrate efforts on one or two methods that can be adapted to suit almost all belays likely to be encountered and to consolidate these skills throughout the day's climbing. Be consistent in the techniques you teach and the student will grasp the principles of safe stance organisation more rapidly. This will make your task easier and allow you to introduce variants as and when appropriate.

Given an ideal stance, you would try to bring anchors together to one central point. Unless the anchor is a sturdy tree or huge block or a fixed anchor, you will always need more than one point to make a solid anchor. The simplest way to bring two anchor points together is to connect the two with a sling.

Photo 2 shows the basic set-up very clearly. (There are other ways illustrated in vol. one, page 122.) By tying an overhand in the sling you effectively create two separate slings. Make sure that you clip into both with a screwgate krab when tying yourself to the anchor.

This system is very simple yet efficient. Problems may occur if the two anchors that you select are too far apart to connect them with a standard long sling. As the angle increases at the point in which you tie into the anchor, the less evenly distributed is the load on each anchor. If the angle between the two anchor points is 90 degrees or less the load will be distributed equally 50% to each. After 90 degrees the loading increases by an undetermined amount and at 120 degrees the load each anchor must bear is the full 100%. Two anchors are normally selected because one alone is not sufficient to hold the force of a fall and it is therefore advantageous to distribute the load so that each has less to hold in the event of a fall. An angle of 120 degrees is obviously undesirable as the anchors must each bear the full force of any any load. This is unsatisfactory if you have chosen multiple anchors because you are not confident that one alone will be able to hold the full force of any load. Many instructors now carry huge slings for just such an eventuality. This is all very well, but they are awkward for clients to carry and, unless you are going to encourage all your students to use one for their own climbing, it may not be a valuable learning experience.

Two normal sized long slings might be a more appropriate method to use. If one is too long it can be shortened to the correct length by tying a knot in it. You might also consider using a snake sling.

The alternative method of tying in to two anchors is to use the rope. Clearly, anchors that are a long way apart will take up quite a bit of rope, but what you will be teaching is a method that is applicable to use outside of an instructional day and one that the students will certainly need to know if they hope to climb on their own in the future.

In terms of stance organisation it is simpler to bring two anchors to one point using a sling. If you decide to use the rope method you will need to think much more carefully about how you position everyone on the stance. It is very easy to get in a terrible tangle!

It is very difficult to set standard procedures applicable to all stances, but there are principles that apply to almost all possible variances.

Always try to position your stance so that you are able to see clients on the whole pitch, including the stance that you leave them on. Sometimes this will mean that you have to ignore stances as recommended in the guidebook description of the route and take intermediate ones. This is particularly important if you think that your clients may experience difficulties in climbing the route. If you can see them, you will be able to encourage them and talk them through a sequence of moves. You will also be able to keep an eye on them to check that they release themselves from the belay correctly. You will also be better placed to prevent problems occurring, such as climbing past a runner without unclipping from it. Furthermore, they themselves will feel encouraged that you are able to keep a close eye on them throughout and they will know that they can ask for help whenever it might be needed.

Position yourself on the stance so that each client can arrive without having to climb over or under ropes attached to the anchor and so that they have as much room as possible to stand or sit comfortably.

Consider the order and direction in which you will move off on to the next pitch. If the climb goes to one side or the other try to arrange things so that they will leave the stance in the correct sequence. This will avoid any possible tangles. When you ask them to clip into the anchor point or points, do so in a sequence that is clear for them to understand. Photo 24 shows a suggested set-up.

If you are going to ask the second to belay the third you will need to make sure that you yourself are in a position to supervise and to act as a safety back up by holding the controlling rope in a way that allows you to lock it off correctly in case they are unable to hold a falling second. This is particularly important if you are instructing novices on their first experiences of multi-pitch climbing.

You will also need to make sure that the ropes are well organised and will run off the pile smoothly and free of tangles as folk climb away from the stance. This is sometimes the most onerous of tasks. It is not so much of a problem if there is a large enough ledge on which to store the ropes, but if you have a small, cramped stance there may not be sufficient room and you might have to lap coil the ropes over a spike or over the rope to the anchor. (See chapter 8 for hanging stances, p. 367). Here again, make sure that the ropes are arranged in the sequence in which they need to run off – your end off the top of one pile and the rope attached to the middle person off the top of the other.

Stance organisation with two clients requires considerable practice and a methodical approach. Try to do as much of it as possible prior to assessment, as it is an aspect of the MIA that candidates frequently fail to do competently.

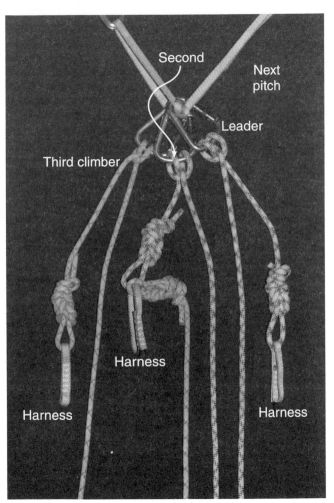

24 Stance organisation. Arrange everyone so that it is straightforward to move off on the next pitch.

## CLIMBING IN PARALLEL OR SERIES

Traditional climbing is conducted in series, that is to say only one person climbs at a time. Guided climbing is sometimes done in parallel, when the guide or instructor trails two ropes, one attached to each client. Both clients will climb at the same time one slightly behind the other. The distinct advantage of this latter method is one of speed.

Any instructional day out should be conducted in series. The reasons for this are simple enough – you are teaching people to climb in a traditional manner and should teach by example rather than use techniques that your clients or students are unlikely to use or even need. The only exception might be when there is a need to move more quickly due to the lateness of the hour or incoming bad weather.

Guiding on the other hand is slightly different in that the emphasis must be placed on climbing as much rock as is humanly possible in a day! To this end you will benefit from the advantage of the extra speed gained by both clients climbing at the same time. But that is the only benefit.

It can be quite unpleasant for the clients if they are in each other's way or their ropes become entangled and there are additional complexities to be dealt with by yourself as the leader.

The least complex climbs to cope with are those that are straight up and down. Ropes will run perfectly and you will be able to protect each client with the rope running directly to them. Unfortunately, not all climbs are so accommodating and anything that involves any kind of diagonal or horizontal traverse will necessitate the placement of strategic runners in order to keep the ropes running as you would like them to. This poses a dilemma. Should you clip each rope into every runner or have separate runners for each (photo 25)? Should you ask one person to belay you on one or both ropes or do you ask each client to belay you on their own rope?

25 Climbing in parallel. Note how the ropes run separately for ease of unclipping from runners.

The answers to these questions vary according to the nature of the climbing. You may decide to clip both ropes into all the runners via the same karabiner. Unfortunately what tends to happen is that ropes frequently get crossed over when the first client arrives at the runner to remove their rope. Better to use a separate quick draw for each rope that you clip into the runner. This means that you have to carry lots of quick draws or reduce the numbers of runners placed on the pitch.

If you decide to place runners alternately on separate ropes you should, for safety sake, ask each client to belay you on their own rope. Placing runners this way may not allow you to position them in the most ideal situation for the client's protection. Remember that runners are placed for three reasons – one is for personal safety in case you fall, the other is for the directional safety of your clients whilst they are climbing, and the third is to show the way.

You will need to decide how best to belay your clients whilst they are climbing. In doing so you have to consider the worst case scenario where you might have both clients hanging on the rope at the same time. Unlikely though this might be, it is nonetheless a possibility.

In order to hold them effectively you must have a good stance with good anchors and arrange the belaying system so that you will not have to bear the full weight of both should they fall at the same time. You can use a belay device attached to your central tie on loop on the harness, just as you would for climbing in series, but you must position yourself so that the load is transferred directly on to the anchors.

You might choose to use a direct belaying method where the belay device is attached directly to the anchor and you attach yourself independently, either to another anchor or to the main one. It is clear that if you elect to use such a method, the anchors have to be a hundred per cent reliable as they will bear the full weight of a fallen climber. However many anchors you use, you will need to bring them to one central point at which you attach the belay device.

The type of belay method you use on a direct belay demands careful consideration. A belay device such as the ATC, BUG or variable controller can only be operated correctly if you stand behind it and are able to lock it off if the need arises. A figure eight descendeur can be operated from below quite effectively, though for maximum braking effect the controlling rope should be kept behind the device.

The New Alp belay plate is designed specifically for this type of belaying. Photo 26 shows the correct way to set up the plate on a direct belay. Unfortunately, as a belay device it does have its drawbacks. It is very difficult to pay out any rope if you want to give slack or if a climber wants to move down to a resting place. If there is any weight on the device it is virtually impossible to pay out rope, or to take in the unloaded rope. This means that if you have one client who has fallen off on to the rope, the other must stop climbing as you cannot take in any more rope through the plate and cannot therefore assure their safety.

On the positive side, the device locks off very effectively and there is never any doubt about holding a fallen climber. It is also possible to leave clients attached to the plate directly to the anchor, eliminating the need for them to tie into it separately. It is advisable to tie off the rope as shown in photo 27, to provide additional security.

When climbing in parallel you are quite likely to experience one other major problem – that of ropes getting twisted. This happens when clients need to step over or go under the other's rope. Whatever the reasons might be for this, and indeed there are few, it happens more regularly than is desirable. To prevent it happening at all will demand that you keep a very close eye on your clients and make sure that if, for whatever reason, they have to cross ropes, they do so without introducing a twist into the system.

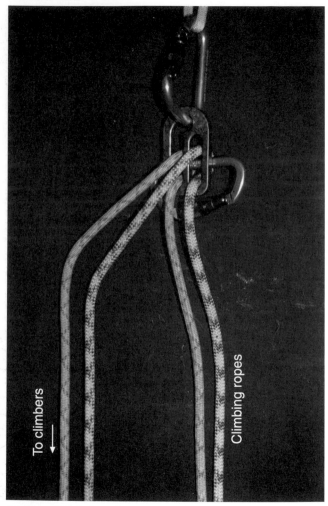

To climbers

Climbing ropes

26 New Alp belay plate.

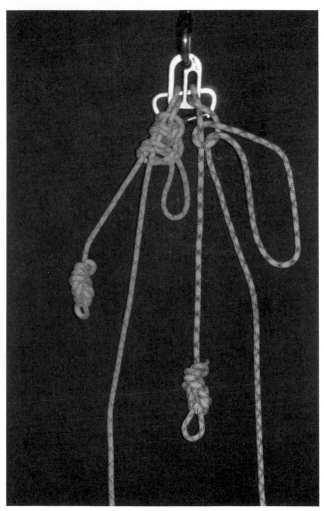

27 Tying off the New Alp belay plate.

Any twists can most easily be sorted out on arrival at the stance and should be taken out as soon as is reasonably possible before more accumulate and create all manner of other problems.

Climbing in series is subject to far fewer idiosyncrasies and is the preferred method of climbing, but it is as well to practise parallel climbing for the occasions when it may be more applicable.


## TEACHING LEAD CLIMBING

Anyone who teaches rock climbing will at some time or other need to instruct the skills required to lead rock climbs safely. It is an important element of the MIA and one that you may be asked to demonstrate at assessment.

Before you encourage or permit anyone to practise leading you must first establish that the students are capable and that they have a desire to lead. The decision to allow them to lead must be based on their ability to operate a belay device correctly, particularly as a second safeguarding a leader, and to have a good understanding of the principles of arranging anchors and running belays. Finally you must explain to them that being in the lead on a climb does carry certain risks, particularly of falling, and that there has to be an acceptance of this by the students before you can go ahead. It may even be worth trying to stage a falling leader scenario in a very safe situation or, of course, to use a special weight drop machine where a leader fall can be simulated.

Anyone who leads for the first time, no matter if they have followed climbs of HVS or even harder, must undertake climbs that are technically well within their ability. This is necessary to ensure the highest margin of safety possible. As a rough guide, someone who follows VS 4c competently ought perhaps to begin on a Diff or at most a V Diff climb.

There are different ways to conduct the teaching of lead

climbing. A gradual introduction might take the form of the student clipping into pre-placed runners whilst being top roped. As a progression from this, strategic runners might be pre-placed with the student placing their own in between. Any time a student places running belays, the instructor must be present to assist and advise and to give the final go ahead to use a particular placement or not.

Clearly it is advantageous to try to run a runner placement session from the ground using whatever cracks and features might be available.

When the concept of introducing students to lead climbing was instigated, it was accepted practice for the instructor to solo the climb alongside the student. The instructor would carry a short length of rope with a screwgate krab attached to the end. This rope would either be coiled around the body or carried in a bum bag around the waist. The idea was that it would be a quick and simple method of getting a rope to a student in difficulty – all very well if you can arrange a runner quickly, send the rope down, clip it into the student's harness and attach it to the runner with an Italian hitch, all in the space of a few seconds!

This method, whilst adhered to for many years, is clearly flawed. The instructor is exposed to considerable risk. Even though they might be climbing on ground that is well within the margins of their ability, an accidental stumble or slip cannot be ruled out. If an instructor were to fall they might knock off the student or, at worst, fall and be killed, leaving inexperienced climbers on the crag without the necessary knowledge of how to proceed.

Apart from that most obvious risk, on many climbs there are not enough good holds for instructor and student to share. It might mean in some cases that the instructor is off to one side on VS ground, while the student is on V Diff ground. This, of course, is the worst possible scenario!

Whilst this technique is still used by a very few instructors, by far the most commonly used system of introducing lead climbing is for the instructor to climb the pitch and fix a rope in place at the stance at the end of the pitch, abseil down and then to jumar up the rope by the side of the student who is leading. (See chapter 9, page 380, for techniques of ascending a fixed rope.)

The instructor might place a few strategic running belays on the way up and leave these in for the student. Being attached to a mechanical ascending device allows the instructor complete freedom of movement at all times – to be at the side of the student or slightly above. This level of security is both a confidence booster for the student and also permits the instructor to help out more readily in case of difficulty.

It is a good idea to rig some kind of safety back up for the student that allows the instructor to clip them in if they are finding things difficult or if they decide that they do not feel confident about climbing too far above a runner. This safety back up can be arranged simply enough by attaching a long sling to the ascending device (or a second device) and making sure that there is a screwgate krab in the end which can be clipped into the student's harness quickly and simply when needed. Photo 28 shows a suggested set-up.

Many instructors will take the trouble to back up the ascending device either with a French prusik or a second device. The combination of something like a jumar with a Ropeman above it works particularly well.

The student who is belaying the leader must be well secured and their anchor should almost always include one that is capable of taking an upward pull. (There are exceptions to this rule, of course, and one that springs readily to mind is that of a heavyweight second attached to a great big solid spike above their shoulder level.) If the lead student falls there is then no chance whatsoever that the belayer will be pulled off the stance and you can be assured that they will be able to concentrate all efforts on holding the rope securely.

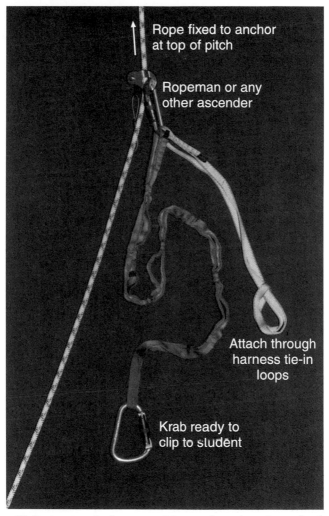

28 Instructor rig for supervising students learning to lead.

As you ascend the rope alongside the lead student you will be able to stop and discuss runner placement and offer tips on how to place them better, or things to consider if extending runners – or any other words of wisdom you are able to impart.

Running belays should be placed at fairly close intervals. Not only will this increase margins of safety but it will also concentrate the practice of placement, giving the student many opportunities to place gear. The first runner off the ground or off a stance should be placed by the instructor and the student's rope clipped into it before moving off on the climb. On stances part way up a climb this will avoid the possibility that a fall factor 2 (see below) might occur if the student where to fall off immediately above the stance and without a runner in place.

On arrival at a stance you can also supervise the selection and setting up of anchors.

As students gain more experience and confidence at leading you can step aside more often and allow them that most valuable of all learning experiences – self-discovery. Knowing that you are on hand to correct mistakes will be a huge confidence boost to the student.

If both of your students have a desire to lead you can allow them to lead through. Before leading the next pitch you will need to go up yourself and fix the rope in place that you are going to ascend on.

It is clear that at this stage of a rock climbing student's progress you are getting much closer to the time when they will be able to take care of themselves. Though it doesn't apply to everyone who takes up rock climbing, this surely has to be the ultimate objective for the instructor – and one of the most gratifying.

*Notes on Fall Factor*

*This is a theoretical measure of the forces involved in a leader fall. I say theoretical because there are many external influences to consider that may reduce the forces likely to be experienced.*

*The maximum fall factor that can be reached is 2. At this level ropes and equipment might be expected to fail. (There are circumstances where it may be greater but these are not necessarily applicable at this level.) I once had the misfortune to experience a fall factor 2 and can tell you it isn't at all pleasant.*

*The fall factor is worked out simply by dividing the length of a fall by the amount of rope paid out. For example, a leader who is 3 m (10 ft) above the second and who falls off before arranging a runner will fall 6 m (20 ft). This gives a fall factor of 2. However, this high factor will only be reached if the rock is vertical or overhanging and there is no absorption of the shock loading in the system (rope stretch, climbers bodies and friction over the rock etc.) which is why it is really only a theoretical measure. Nonetheless, all climbers should be aware of the problem, and instructors particularly. Ensuring that there is a solid runner as soon as possible after leaving the stance will avoid the possibility of a direct loading of fall factor 2 onto the belayer.*

*Interestingly, big falls at the end of a long pitch are quite acceptable! Take the following example. Rope out 40 m (130 ft), last runner at 30 m (100 ft), length of fall = 20 m (65 ft). Fall Factor 0.5! You'd have time to experience the full pleasures of flying during a 20 m (65 ft) fall.*

29 Learning to lead with an instructor in close attendance.

# 6  Short Roping for MIA

This is probably the aspect of MIA that proves to be the downfall of many of those who fail at assessment. The reasons for this centre on a lack of understanding of the technique and the context in which it is intended to fit within the MIA scheme.

This confusion is possibly because there are a number of techniques that fit broadly into the same category. In 1994, in an attempt to clarify the differing styles and to put a name to each, I proposed the following which have subsequently become widely accepted definitions.

## CONFIDENCE ROPING

To safeguard an individual within a hillwalking group who would gain a boost of confidence in an apparently exposed situation by being tied to a short length of rope which is held by the instructor or leader. The instructor may not even tie into the rope. Both will usually move at the same time, therefore not impeding the progress of the group as a whole. The use of the rope is normally unplanned.

## SHORT ROPING

The use of the rope to safeguard one or two clients in ascent or descent on terrain that is exposed and where a slip could have serious consequences. The terrain is not continuous rock climbing or scrambling but may have short sections of technical difficulty approaching the V Diff grade ( or exceptionally, even Severe). Sections that require safeguarding will generally be very short but could be anything from a few metres to 20 m (65 ft) or a little more. The instructor or leader will climb the section of difficulty first leaving the clients secure on a ledge.

Normally clients will move over the difficult ground at the same time, tied a few feet apart on the climbing rope. The instructor will safeguard them, using suitable belaying techniques that do not impede efficient and speedy ascent or descent. These techniques are likely to be direct belay methods or, where suitable, a braced stance with waist or shoulder belay. The whole party will move at the same time between sections of difficulty and in less exposed situations.

Occasionally in descent it may be appropriate to lower the clients, either individually or exceptionally both together.

The leader or instructor will not normally place running belays for his or her own protection but may do so for directional stability in safeguarding the clients.

## MOVING TOGETHER

The party will travel at the same time over terrain that presents a combination of exposure and continuous technical difficulty or extreme exposure alone. Most commonly this technique is linked with moving along alpine ridges or mixed climbs where speed with a degree of safety is preferable. A competent and compatible rope of two will move together with the rope tight between them at all times. For safety, the first climber on the rope will arrange running belays at suitable intervals. It is hoped that these running belays will go some way towards preventing a tragedy should one or both climbers fall. On arriving at anything of greater difficulty the party will stop and initiate normal climbing procedures.

In a professional scenario where one is caring for a client or clients the position is much more tenuous and requires sound judgement, quick decision processes and sharp reactions that can only be gained through much experience and training at a high level. Consequently this style of safeguarding a client or clients in the mountains is normally the preserve of the guide and not appropriate at MIA.

From the above, it is clear that the domain that fits the MIA is in between that of guide and that of mountain walking leader.

There are two mountain scenarios where the technique is applicable at this level. One is during the approach to or descent from a rock climb and the other is when a day out in the mountains is planned to include a scramble. The techniques and principles are the same for both scenarios. It might be appropriate to begin by outlining the reasons for using short roping and to explain what the principles are.

Scrambling terrain, either in ascent or descent, will undoubtedly feature climbing that requires the use of both hands. It may also take place in exposed situations where there is a very real risk of serious injury or worse in the event of a fall. Usually the climbing is not of a high technical standard, though moss- and lichen-covered rock in the pouring rain will make even simple climbing difficult. As stated before, any sections of actual climbing may be very short and interspersed with other sections of very easy terrain.

Clearly, this type of terrain does not require the use of a more traditional approach of pitching and making stances because it would slow the party down too much. It is preferable therefore to have the rope in place, with everyone tied on to it, so that it can be used as and when required.

The overriding principle is to make sure that the use of the rope provides a good balance of safety but without slowing down progress. To implement this efficiently you must be flexible enough that you can adapt to any type of terrain and use effective belay techniques where appropriate.

Furthermore, you will gain advantages of both efficiency and safety if you remain close to your clients and maintain eye to eye contact throughout. Much can be learnt about the way people react to any given situation and such understanding may forewarn of any impending problem. Such non-verbal communication is worth more in some respects than all the knowledge of ropework acquired.

## TYING ON TO THE ROPE

You will not need to use the whole length of the rope but you must ensure that you can vary the length quickly. To do this you will need to coil the rope around your body and tie it off, so that it can be released when necessary. A simple way to tie off the rope is illustrated in photo 81 in vol. one. An alternative method is shown in photos 30, 31 and 32. The method illustrated here is very quickly undone to let out more rope, yet provides an effective locking system so that if you have to take a load directly around the coils it will not tighten up around the shoulders. However, it does have drawbacks, most notably that it will tighten up around your body if you, as the leader, take a fall. This is, of course, the worst case scenario, but if it were to happen, tying off the rope in this way might cause unnecessary injury and jeopardise the safety of your clients.

Some people like to tie off the rope at intervals, so that when you have to drop coils you do so only up to the next tie off point. This is very convenient in some respects but does mean that you have a bulky bunch of knots around your harness tie in point.

Those in your care should be tied into the rope. One person on the end and any others should be tied in with an isolation loop. Avoid, if you can, tying in people directly to the harness abseil loop with a karabiner. This loop is intended to take a static load only and, although it is immensely strong, the manufacturer does not recommend clipping a climbing rope in with a krab directly.

Better to tie an overhand knot in a bight of rope creating a loop about 1.5 m (5 ft) long to form the isolation loop. Then tie a second overhand knot a little more than .5 m (1½ ft) from the end of the loop. Thread the loop through the harness tie on points and re-thread the overhand to create a secure tie on. The end of the loop can be clipped back into the harness for extra safety (photos 33 and 34). It used to be fashionable to use an

30 Alternative tie off for short roping: Stage 1.

31 Alternative tie off for short roping: Stage 2.

32 Alternative tie off for short roping: Stage 3.

Alpine butterfly to create the isolation loop, but in recent years the overhand has become the favourite. It is an equally strong knot and has the advantage that it can be adjusted more easily to vary the length of the isolation loop and can even be tied or untied without removing the rope from those you are safeguarding.

The distance that you have between the clients will depend largely on the type of ground you are moving over. As a general guideline about 2 m (6½ ft) is just right. Any more, and you will find that slack will easily develop between them, but any less will mean that one is trying to avoid standing on the other's fingers. It is difficult to say exactly how many people you can have on the rope in this way. Much depends on the nature of the terrain. The more people you have, the harder it becomes to manage. One is perfect. Two is ideal, three is manageable, but any more and one must ask the question whether or not margins of safety are compromised.

## METHODS OF SAFEGUARDING THE PARTY

At every difficulty encountered you must safeguard the members of your party adequately. The key here is to have a number of differing methods at your disposal so that you are able to adapt efficiently to each situation as it is presented. There are no rules of thumb to apply, other than to be safe. The simplest method of safeguarding someone is to take a braced stance and either to take in the rope through your hands or use a shoulder belay. The success and safety of this method is tenuous to say the least. Much will depend on how strong you are and how heavy your clients might be. A diminutive person may not be able to hold a person weighing 80 kilos with the rope running through their hands.

A secure braced stance (photo 35) is the foundation stone to this technique. You must not stand casually on the edge of a ledge and expect to hold someone who slips. You have to lean

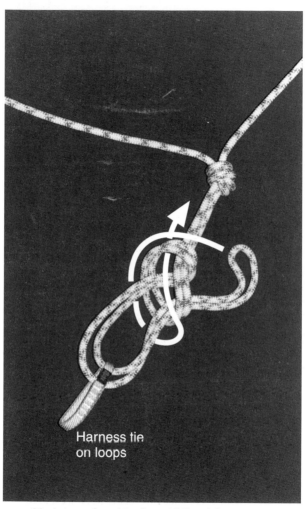

Harness tie
on loops

33 An overhand in the middle of the rope: Stage 1.

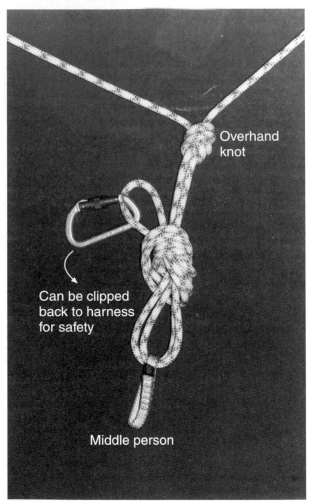

Overhand knot

Can be clipped back to harness for safety

Middle person

34 An overhand in the middle of the rope: Stage 2.

back against the rock or sit down or wedge yourself behind a substantial boulder. 'Every foothold must be a belay' is a popular expression of a colleague of mine. And he's right – think of it like that and you'll not go far wrong.

It is a good idea to use leather gloves that allow you a more positive grip on the rope. If you decide to take in the rope directly through your hands, keep it tight all the time. You should almost pull the client up, but without making them feel that you are giving too much assistance, for they may find it disconcerting.

Keeping the rope tight in this way will enable you to correct a slip quickly before it develops into a fall. This reaction zone is a vital part of any short roping or moving together scenario.

If you feel the need for extra security and holding power you can use a shoulder belay or waist belay. Photos in vol. one, pages 67 and 70 show this clearly. If using the shoulder belay, always remember to have the loaded rope coming underneath the armpit and the dead rope over the opposite one. It is paramount that you do not lean forward because any loading of the rope will pull it off your shoulders. Lean back slightly and dig your feet well in.

It is not advisable to use this braced stance approach on ground that has a high degree of exposure nor where steep scrambling or graded climbing is encountered. Better to employ it where difficulties are short, there is a good ledge below and a spacious one to stand on and the angle is low. For more technical ground and where sections requiring the security of the rope are longer you should use a direct belaying method. These take a little longer to set up than a braced stance and require an element of judgement and imagination.

The simplest form of direct belay is to take the rope in around a flake or spike of rock. It may be obvious, but needs to be said, that the anchor must be a hundred per cent solid. If it isn't and it fails under load the consequences could be

35 A well-braced stance with extra friction generated by
running the rope over a boulder.

catastrophic. Many people fail at assessment for selecting anchors that are clearly not safe. Try to ensure that there are no sharp edges that might cause unnecessary abrasion of the rope. If there are it may be preferable to use a sling instead. Flakes and spikes are the most obvious things to use as direct belays, but sometimes you might find it possible to use other rock features. For example, a large rounded boulder could be used by climbing over to the opposite side from where you anticipate the load will come. The rope running over the rock will generate friction which will help you to hold any load. Small nubbins of rock might also be used provided that they are part of the mountain and not something that is held on with a bit of mud or grass.

Avoid anything that has a pronounced V-shape that the rope might jam up in. Not only might it jam it might also cut the rope if it comes under load.

A sling and Italian hitch can also be used where you feel the need for a more reliably smooth-running direct belay. If you decide to take this option, make sure that you use an HMS karabiner for the Italian hitch. D-shaped krabs hinder the free running of the rope in an Italian hitch and make taking in and paying out troublesome (photo 36).

Bringing the clients up is a straightforward affair. Make sure that you keep a grip on the controlling rope at all times. Any momentary lapse of concentration in this may catch you unprepared to hold a fall. (See photos 40, 41 42 and 43 for the taking in sequence around a direct belay. The same principles apply to taking in through an Italian hitch attached to a sling around the anchor.)

On stances in exposed positions where someone might fall off a ledge, you must secure the party somehow. You must certainly consider your own personal safety for, though you might be quite at ease standing on the edge of a ledge over a big drop, you are still responsible for your clients' safety and that means your own too. Consider clipping in to the anchor

36 Direct belay using an Italian hitch.

using a long cow's tail at the very least in exposed situations (photo 37).

When those you are safeguarding arrive at the stance you will need to have planned your actions in advance. The first person to arrive will be well protected but unless you are prepared for looking after the second or subsequent members, they will be unprotected whilst you secure the first.

There are a number of different courses of action. You can tie off the first person to arrive by securing them around the direct belay. This is done by wrapping the rope several times around the anchor or by tying the dead rope back into their harness. Or you can keep hold of the main rope whilst reaching down to take the rope between the first and second client and then drape it over the direct belay anchor. This is referred to as a counter-balance belay. Provided that the rope sits well down below the top of the anchor and is not likely to get accidentally flicked off, two people can be left on a stance securely in this way.

If you are using an Italian hitch you will find it easier to have a second HMS krab on the sling into which you can clip the rope between the clients (photo 38). To do this efficiently you will need to be very adept at tying knots with one hand (photos 39a and b). Either tie an Italian hitch or clip them directly into the anchor with a clove hitch. Once clipped in the clove hitch can be adjusted so that everyone is tight to the anchor (photos 38 and 39).

Very occasionally you may need to implement the more traditional belaying method of making a stance and using a belay device. If you need to do this it will obviously impede speedy progress and so must only be used in exceptional circumstances where you feel that the party might be exposed to greater risk than is usual on scrambling terrain.

All these procedures take time to implement. The real skill is to minimise the time taken so that efficient movement up the scramble is assured.

37 Direct belay using an Italian hitch. The instructor is secured separately.

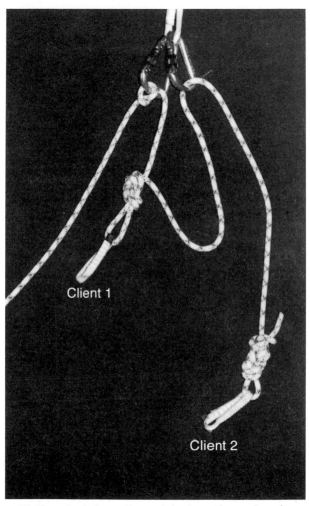

Client 1

Client 2

38  Counter balance through krab on the anchor sling.

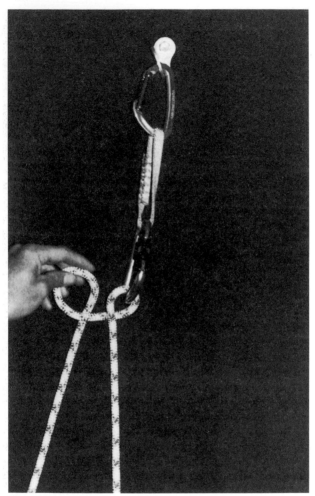

39a  Tying a clove hitch with one hand: Stage 1.

39b Tying a clove hitch with one hand: Stage 2

40 Taking in the rope using a direct belay: Stage 1. Note that the same sequence applies to the Italian hitch.

41 Taking in the rope using a direct belay: Stage 2.

42 Taking in the rope using a direct belay: Stage 3.

43 Stage 4: go back to Stage 1.

When you arrive at easy sections where people can move without risk or walk to the next bit of difficulty, you can take up the slack rope in coils and carry them in your hand. To do this, coil the rope up in short coils, no more than a foot or so long, beginning at your own tie on point and finishing about a metre or so from the first person down the rope. By coiling this way you are able to drop coils as you need to. (See photos on page 182, vol. one.)

## GOING DOWN

Descents using short roping techniques present their own problems. The principles of safeguarding the rope with either a braced stance or a direct belay apply in the same way as for going up.

The main difference is one of route finding. If you know the way down well, this is not so much of a problem, as you can explain to people where they must go. If, however, you are on unfamiliar territory you will undoubtedly need to explore the line to take yourself.

This must be done without the need for you to go first. You cannot safeguard the party well enough from below even if you place running belays. It must be done always from above. To this end experience at seeing and deciding on a route pays dividends. It is unlikely that those in your care will have the necessary experience to choose their own route down.

The difficulties are compounded by the fact that you may need to secure the clients whilst you yourself are descending. To do this you'll need to allow them to make themselves secure. In order to keep a close eye on folk whilst they are doing this you should ensure that they do not get too far below you. Much better to descend in very short stages where you can see what is happening and give instructions as appropriate.

Occasionally it may be preferable to lower people down. If you have a sound anchor, then you might consider lowering both at the same time. Usually you would only do this on relatively low angled terrain where people can support much of their own weight and where you can see them at all times.

If the ground you are lowering down is steep, or involves an overhang, or is at all problematical, lower your clients one at a time.

A way to do this is to untie the middle person from the rope and undo their knot. Make sure before you do this that they are safe, either well back from the edge and unanchored, or clipped to an anchor with a cow's tail. (See photo 21 chapter 5.)

Lower the person on the end of the rope down. If you still have lots of rope available, tie on the second person just below the lowering device and then lower them down to join their partner. You may then be able to climb down or abseil off, using the remainder of the rope which can be retrieved once you are down by untying from the end and pulling it down around the anchor.

If you find that there is insufficient rope to effect this you will have to ask the person you lowered down first to untie from the rope so that you can haul it back up and lower the second.

Very rarely you may decide to abseil. Arrange folk in the usual way for a stacked abseil. You descend first and call each of your clients down when you are ready for them. See chapter 5.

Short roping requires considerable practice before you can do it well. This practice needs to take place in a real situation where you genuinely have to take care of others. It requires those that use it to make a great many decisions based on judgement and familiarity with this type of terrain and the use of appropriate rope techniques.

# 7 Sport Climbs and Climbing Walls

*Some safety considerations*

Doesn't it always feel pretty safe climbing on bolts? Clipping in to a sturdy chunk of metal fixed deep into the rock induces a feeling of immortality and encourages bigger air time. It allows you to concentrate on the finer points of style and technique and to push always that little bit further . . . The final lunge for the chain lower off or belay is something positive to aim for – a haven at last after the vertical onslaught.

Sport climbing, as it is known the world over, has become one of the most popular aspects of the sport of rock climbing – and justly so. The feel good factor of safety widens the appeal for the less brave, it requires less equipment and, furthermore, one is able to push physical capabilities beyond what might otherwise be achievable on traditional climbs where protection and belays may be sparse or inadequate.

Not wishing to put a dampener on the reverie of such delights, have you ever stopped to think carefully about the things that might possibly go wrong? How problems might be avoided or solved? There are very few things to go awry, it's true, but here are one or two that might give you cause for concern the next time you're contemplating taking a big flight on to a single bolt runner . . . Consider clipping a single screwgate krab into the first bolt. If it's not too far off the ground and you need the protection for the first few hard moves you'll probably be thankful for a short connection to stop you from hitting the ground in an early fall. The benefits of doing this however come into play when you are higher up the climb. Clipping in securely to the first bolt will help to ensure that the rope runs correctly through all subsequent runners. It also creates extra friction in the event of a big plummet, enabling the second to maintain a more secure grip on the rope.

Everyone has their own favourite way of racking gear, clipping into bolts and clipping the rope in to the quick draw. It is worth paying a little attention to one or two points. Firstly, consider the direction in which you will be moving once you have clipped the bolt. As a *general* rule it's advisable to have the gates of both krabs facing away from the direction of movement. This will ensure that the load comes correctly on to the back, load-bearing, axis of the krabs. Any possibility that the load may come across the weakest axis or along the gate side of the krab is to be avoided at all costs.

There have been exceptional circumstances, particularly with bent gate krabs, were a fall has resulted in the rope catching in the bend of the gate and actually unclipping itself when the load came on to the rope. The possibility of this occurring is greatly heightened if you clip the rope directly to the krab on the bolt. If you need to clip the rope directly into a bolt, without using a quick draw, you'd be well advised to use a D-shaped screwgate, which is much stronger.

Make sure that the quick draw is not twisted in any way. If it is, it might cause a similar twisting action in the event of a fall.

All these problems can be avoided by very simple preparation before leaving the ground. Rack up all the quick draws with krabs facing the same way – it will help too, if you fix the bent gate krab with a strong rubber band. These can be bought or improvised with ordinary elastic bands, castrating rings or sticky tape. It is also possible to buy quick draws with captive eye loops for the attachment of karabiners and these are well worthy of consideration.

There are two methods of karabiner to quick draw attachment. Both are illustrated in photo 44 and both are equally acceptable. The only common denominator is to ensure that

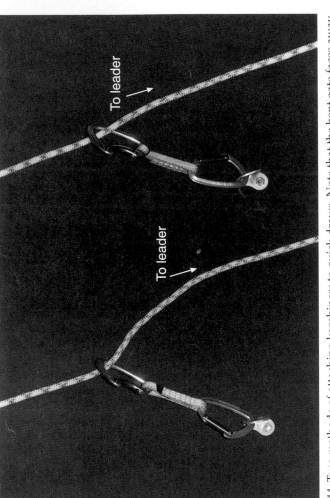

To leader

To leader

44 Two methods of attaching karabiners to quick draws. Note that the bent gate faces away from the direction of travel.

the opening end of each krab is always away from the quick draw.

Repeated falls on to bolts may damage the krabs that attach the quick draw to the bolt. Such damage may be seen as burrs or ridges in the krab and, in worst cases, a distinct thinning of the metal may be apparent. This is a particular problem with the more common hanger, as seen in photo 44. Eco bolts and large ring bolts, such as those found on the Continent, present less of a sharp profile. It is advisable to use much sturdier krabs directly on to bolts, as these will last considerably longer if fallen on regularly. If you have any doubts about the safety of your equipment it should be discarded.

Burrs in the bend of krabs can also cause a good deal of damage to quick draws. Repeated falls whilst dogging a climb may cause abrasion of the nylon, with an associated weakening of the quick draw, to the extent that it might snap unexpectedly. Conscientious checking of your rack and changing damaged bits promptly will go a long way to preventing serious accidents.

## CLIPPING BOLTS

By arranging your quick draws in some semblance of order you will be able to maximise efficiency and, as a result, will waste less energy clipping the bolt and then the rope into the quick draw. Better to reserve strength for the climb than fumble around trying to disentangle gear from your harness or turn krabs around in bolts or quick draws.

Clipping the rope into a quick draw requires a certain amount of dexterity which is easily achieved with practice. Like so many things, there is more than one way to do this. The following is a suggestion only and I'm sure that as you gain experience, you will adapt or develop your own style.

Photos 45 and 46 illustrate the following suggestion. Bring up the rope draped over your thumb and middle finger to the

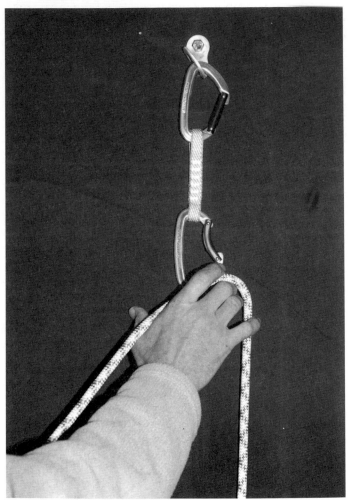

45 Clipping the climbing rope into a quick draw: Stage 1.

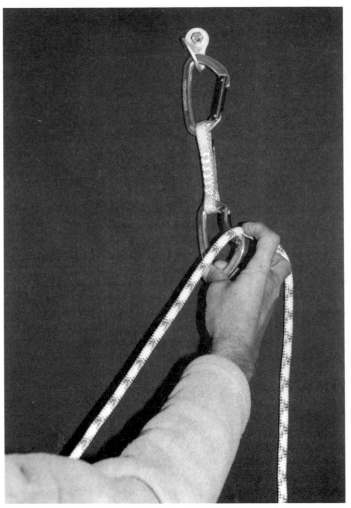

46 Clipping the climbing rope into a quick draw: Stage 2.

krab. Hook your ring finger into the bottom of the krab and pull it under a small amount of tension – this stabilises the krab. Hook the rope into the bent gate and use your forefinger to press the rope into the krab. It takes a milli-second to do this – provided, of course, that your second pays out enough rope!

Remember, too, that bolt hangers can wear out. Particularly ones that are old or made from soft alloy or ones that are subjected to huge numbers of falls – such as those on the crux moves of popular climbs. The unseen part of the bolt can also corrode and weaken over a period of time, though this may not be apparent until it's too late to do anything about it. Be particularly prudent on cliffs near the sea or crags that carry regular seepage. Corrosion occurs mainly on the hidden part of the bolt – that which is buried in the rock.

## LOWERING OFF

Lowering off from the top of the climb rarely poses much of a problem but have you ever thought what you'd do if you dropped the rope whilst threading it through the lower off? Once you get a hold of the lower off, clip yourself in to the anchor with a quick draw. You may want to use a cow's tail with a screwgate krab for safety or a couple of quick draws with the karabiner gates turned in opposite directions. If you only use one quick draw with snaplink krabs be careful not to get into a position where you might untwist the krab connecting you to the anchor. Usually, keeping the quick draw under tension will ensure you remain attached.

To avoid any embarrassment fix the rope to your harness with a krab *before* you untie. Pull up a big loop of slack rope and tie a simple overhand or figure eight knot which can then be clipped with a krab into the gear rack. Untie from the end of the rope, thread it through the lower off and tie back into the end. Don't forget to unclip the rope from the temporary tie off on the gear loop before you ask to be lowered down!

Another very good way of going in to the lower off is described below and illustrated in photo 47. Before you use this method you must be certain that there is more than enough rope to reach the ground safely, as some rope is 'lost' using this system.

On arrival at the lower off, clip in to the anchor entirely independently of the climbing rope. A quick draw between the anchor and the harness abseil loop is the best way. Take the climbing rope and thread it through the lower off as illustrated. Tie a figure eight knot in the loop of rope and clip it in to a screwgate krab on the abseil loop of your harness. *Do not in any circumstances clip it solely through the loop of rope formed by tying on to the end of the climbing rope.*

Having checked that all is in order, undo the tie in knot in the rope end. Pull this through the anchor and get your partner to take your weight on the rope. Unclip from the anchor and ask to be lowered down. The photo should illustrate clearly why you must have slightly more than half the rope available.

Many climbers nowadays choose to use 60-metre, or longer, ropes. In Britain there are few crags that require such a long rope but elsewhere there are many climbs that have 30 m (100 ft) pitches where a long rope is essential.

Remember that if you are very close to the maximum amount of rope available to reach the ground you should ask your belayer to tie in to the other end of the rope or, at the very least, to tie a chunky knot in the end of the rope. This will prevent it sliding through the belay device if the second inadvertently loses a grip on the controlling rope.

Be careful about how you treat lower off anchors. Normally two anchors are provided for the lower off. In the case of Eco bolts these are not connected, as the rope will run freely through them without the need for them to be bought to one central point. Large ring bolts are the same. All other hangers, however, need to be connected, usually with a chunky piece of chain that is connected to the bolts with maillons and the lower

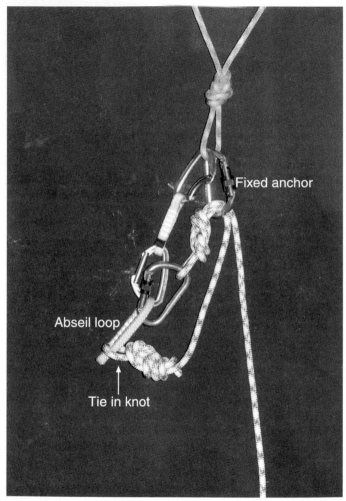

Fixed anchor

Abseil loop

Tie in knot

47 Sequence for lowering off from the top of a sports climb.

off point is either a screwgate krab with the gate glued shut or a large maillon.

Make sure that the lower off is rigged in such a way that if one anchor were to fail the other would remain in place. Occasionally you will arrive at a lower off to discover that it is connected with rope or tape and there is a ring through which to thread the rope. The same principles of guarding against failure apply. Make sure that if one anchor fails the whole lot will not fall apart. If you have any doubts about the set-up, replace the rope or tape with new stuff. Rotted or worn nylon has little strength. *Never ever lower with the rope running over or through a nylon rope or tape sling – the heat generated can easily reach a high enough temperature to melt through the sling.*

Photo 48 shows a suggested method for connecting two anchors together for an abseil point. The same set-up can be utilised as a lower off, though of course you must connect the rope via a krab or a maillon if the rope is to run through. For abseiling off you will probably not want to leave a krab behind and in any case there is no need for one.

## RETRIEVING RUNNERS

If the climb that you have just ascended is very steep, wanders around a little or is overhanging, it can sometimes be a bit problematical retrieving the quick draws from the bolts. You may need to swing around quite a bit and could even find yourself so far out in space that it is impossible to get enough of a swing in to make contact with the rock.

It is a good idea to connect yourself to the rope that runs through the runners which allows you to be lowered down the line of ascent. This is achieved simply enough by connecting a quick draw to the abseil loop of your harness and the other end to the rope through the runners. Photo 49 shows this clearly.

As your partner lowers you down you will almost certainly need to pull yourself along the rope and in towards the next

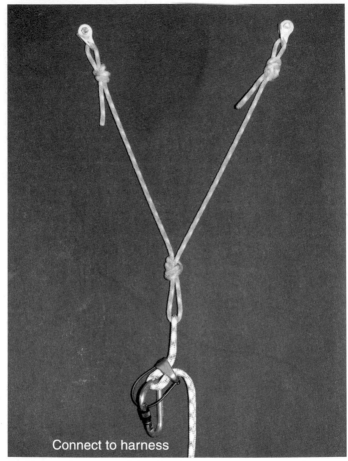

Connect to harness

48 Two anchors rigged for abseil retreat. For re-rigging lower off anchors the same principle applies but clip in a maillon or old krab into the lower loop.

49  De-rigging an overhanging climb. The quick draw
attachment helps maintain contact with the rock.

quick draw to be unclipped. If the rock is really overhanging, it may not be that easy to achieve and any strength that you have left after the climb may wane rapidly just getting the gear out!

When you do make contact with the runner try, if you can, to unclip the quick draw directly from the bolt first, rather than take the rope out. It is likely that you will be holding on tightly to the quick draw, relying on it to hold you in position. If you unclip the rope from the quick draw first and let go of it, the chances are that you will swing out of reach entirely.

The technique requires a bit of practice as it is largely a matter of dexterity, massive strength and quick reaction. Pull yourself in as close as you can to the rock and at the moment you are about to swing out again there will be a milli-second when the quick draw is slack – this is the moment to unclip it. Once released from the bolt, you'll then swing out again into space. If it proves impossible to unclip, you may have to get back on to the rock and release some tension from the rope before you can unclip.

On really overhanging routes you can continue in this way until you reach the last one – in effect, the first that you placed on the ascent. Unclipping from this requires a bit of careful thought. The quick draw that you used to connect yourself to the rope through the runners may have to be released. If you unclip the last quick draw from the bolt without doing this the forces on your belayer will be considerable and may pull them off the ground and, as you swing out, the second could be dragged with you.

Take, for example, the following scenario of a climb that overhangs about 3–4 m (10–15 ft) over its length. The climb begins on a large ledge, below which is a vertical drop of about 10 m (30–35 ft). The second fails to unclip from the lowering rope that runs through the quick draws on the bolts, unclips from the final bolt and takes the b-i-i-i-g swing. The leader is unable to hold the force of the swing and both swing out into the void.

Neither climber is able to regain contact with the rock and they are both left suspended in space without sufficient rope to lower to the ground because the climb used up just under half the rope length, leaving sufficient to regain the ledge but not enough to allow for the extra height of hanging over the crag below the ledge. This is based on a true story!

The problem was solved easily enough, but consider the implications of the second being unable to retain control of the belay device and there being no safety knot in the end of the rope to prevent it sliding through completely. These are lessons learnt the hard way!

## CLIMBING WALL SAFETY

Climbing walls are accessible to all. Their creation is possibly one of the most important developments in climbing history. The number of users increases annually and just about every major conurbation is served by one. Many people who visit walls may only ever climb on walls and may even only try it once. Some will obviously become smitten and progress to climbing outdoors on sport routes and eventually, one would hope, on to traditional climbing.

Because so many users are novices in every respect, including aspects of safety, it is not uncommon to witness a variety of appalling lapses of concentration and rope technique at an indoor climbing venue. It is surprising that so few people are injured seriously. The fact that there are injuries at all is to be lamented, particularly as many indoor accidents can be prevented.

Shoddy belaying technique is perhaps the most commonly witnessed aspect of poor safety technique – particularly when safeguarding someone who is leading a climb.

As with any type of climbing, you are at most risk from injury if you take a fall, either seconding, or particularly leading, close to the ground and most importantly, before you have the first runner clipped. It is a good idea to use an easy way up the first few moves if they are difficult, and clip into the first protection point. You can then descend and try the early hard moves in safety. The belayer should stand close in to the bottom of the wall and as close to the line of the climb without being directly underneath it. If you belay from a distance away from the wall, a falling leader may exert enough force to drag you in towards the foot of the climb. This principle applies equally in 'proper' climbing. In doing so the leader will increase the length of their fall significantly and may hit the ground as a consequence.

The same principle applies as the leader progresses up the climb, though the higher they climb the less chance there is of hitting the ground if a fall occurs. Furthermore, if there are people in the way, milling around at the bottom of the wall or on a climb close by, they might be injured by a falling climber or by a belayer crashing into them.

It is all too easy to be distracted at an indoor venue. Your partner might stop by for a chat, your attention might be captivated by someone doing something hard that you want to do, or you might just aimlessly spend your belaying moments looking around and people watching. Such lapses of concentration on the task in hand might prove to be a catalyst for an accident. It is therefore vitally important to pay close attention at all times.

For this reason you would do well to consider using a belay device designed specifically to make holding a fall much easier. These devices and their methods of application are discussed in Chapter 8.

Consider, too, the weight to weight ratio of the climbing pair. A slight person, weighing in at around 50 kilos (112 lb), will not have much chance of holding a bulkier person of, say, 80 kilos (180 lb) if they take a big fall. Better to ask someone to hold them down or if available, clip them in to an anchor point in the floor or at the base of the wall.

Anyone who takes along a novice to a climbing wall for the first time should spend a good while teaching the rudiments of belaying before embarking on climbs. Many walls now insist that beginners take a short, usually half-hour, session before being let loose on the wall. This is time well spent. In this session not only must you introduce tying on knots and how to operate a belay device, it is also worthwhile giving novices the opportunity to hold a small fall and to lower a climber using a belay device.

# 8 Belaying, Double Rope Technique and Hanging Stances

## BELAYING – LOOKING AFTER THE LEADER

I'm not very good at taking leader falls – I think it has something to do with being brought up on the old ethos 'a leader never falls' or, much more likely, I'm scared to death of flying. A leader who never falls is an uncommon creature these days. In times gone by, before all the trappings of modern protection equipment, a leader simply couldn't afford to fall. If they did it could result in serious injury or much worse. Nowadays it is a somewhat different matter, provided, of course, your runners are sound, you have the nerve to do it and there's someone reliable holding your ropes.

The leader is totally dependant on a good second who is attentive to needs, manipulating the rope, and who can offer moral support in times of stress. It is not always an easy job and, until you are used to handling ropes and understand the principles of what is required of you, it can be something of a tortuous task.

There are a few basic safety principles to consider. Firstly, make sure that you have a secure stance. Many climbers don't bother to anchor themselves at the start of the climb. In normal circumstances this is perfectly OK, but if you are standing on ground that is less than comfortably flat you should consider some sort of anchor to reduce the possibility that you might accidentally stumble backwards and pull the leader off.

If a leader falls off, the second will be subjected to an upward pulling force. The level of this force will be dependant on many different factors. For example, if the rope is running fairly straight up the cliff and the climb is at least vertical, there could be a considerable force generated. A second who is substantially lighter than the leader may well be lifted upwards and might even be lifted a long way off the ground. On the other hand, the force felt by the second may well be insignificant on a climb that meanders around a bit, on which the leader places lots of runners that introduce friction into the system, and is less than vertical, where the fall would be a sliding one.

By far the worst fall that I have ever taken was on a climb called Flashdance on the slate. The climb is quite serious, in that there are few good runners and you have to do a long rising traverse away from small wires. Nearing the end of the traverse things became a little worrying as the realisation dawned on me that a fall might result in hitting the ground. You just have to dispel such worries and commit yourself. Quite by surprise, both my feet slipped at the same time and I found myself sliding earthwards, fingers burning on the slab. The top runner pulled out of the crack and a crash into the ground seemed inevitable. Quick thinking on the part of my second saved the day. By running down the hill he was able to reduce the length of the fall which was a sliding one and relatively slow (!) and I stopped about a couple of metres from the ground. If he'd been anchored to the cliff I would certainly have hit the ground. I didn't go back up for another try!

This example does not mean that it's advisable always to remain unanchored at the bottom of a climb. Rather it is a lesson which might be put to good use on another occasion.

Paying out the rope can be very trying. It isn't so bad if you are climbing on single rope but double ropes are something altogether different. A good second should always try to anticipate when and how much rope the leader is likely to need and when they will need it. I have often watched seconds who don't even pay out the rope at all, relying on the leader actually to drag it through the belay device. If the leader doesn't complain, it's not a problem, but it's much better to give a small loop of slack all the time – not too much though. If you are a leader yourself you will appreciate more the demands that being on the sharp end place upon the climber and should be more sympathetic to the cause.

Leading a climb can become an all absorbing task. When this happens the leader will rely on the second to pay out the right amount of rope at exactly the moment it is needed. Obviously, it helps to anticipate this need if you can see the leader. A leader who is finding things a bit difficult will often become fairly abusive if the second doesn't pay out enough rope at the crucial moment. This is particularly true on hard moves where protection is needed to bolster failing nerve and waning strength. There's nothing worse than trying to drag up the rope to clip it in to a runner and discovering that you can't get enough of it from the second. The worst case is when you almost have enough rope to reach the clip and no more is forthcoming. After a few choice words you are forced to drop the rope for fear that you can't hang on with one hand any more. This, of course, leaves a huge amount of slack in the system which you hope and pray will be taken back in quickly by the second – a nightmare scenario!

Manipulating a rope through a belay device is relatively straightforward for single rope. Remember that you must at all times keep a grip on the locking rope or dead rope. To make things a little easier when you're using two ropes consider the following advice. Always hold the two dead ropes in a closed grip which is slackened, but not released when you need to pay one of the ropes but not the other. The hand that operates the live ropes can be moved freely around and can let go of one rope to pull the other if required. Photos 50 and 51 illustrate a suggested technique. Photo 51 shows a method of maintaining a grip on one rope whilst paying out the other – something to strive for!

Whether you are climbing on double or single rope you should make sure that the rope is in a neat pile and will run

50  Paying out double rope to a leader, one rope at a time.

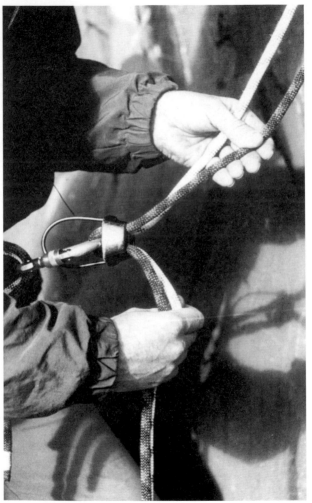

51 When you become more adept, you can hold both whilst paying out one.

smoothly. The all too familiar cry from a second to the leader of 'can you hang on a minute while I sort out this tangle' ought to be an unnecessary one.

The Gri Gri is an excellent device for belaying a leader, though it can of course only be used with single rope. Its only slight disadvantage is that it is heavy to carry. But as it is most commonly used on climbing walls and for sport climbing, this is not really a valid criticism. The device locks automatically when a load is put on the rope. It does this by a very simple cantilever action which grips the rope in a sleeve. There is a handle to release the grip on the rope and this has to be backed up by gripping the dead rope in one hand when lowering. Paying out the rope to the leader is very straightforward and there can be no excuses for not giving enough at the right time! Occasionally the rope will jam if you try to pull it through too quickly. To alleviate this problem make sure that when you want to give rope to the leader you lift the dead or controlling rope above the device (photo 52).

Many people operate the device by gripping the lever which prevents it activating whilst paying out rope, hoping that if the leader falls there will be enough force to activate the locking mechanism (photo 53). In most cases this may work but the certain exception to this is in a slow fall where not much force is felt by the second. The rope can run through the device alarmingly quickly. It should be pointed out that, although this method is used by many climbers, it is not something that the manufacturer recommends.

There are a number of other belay devices available that to a large extent have superseded the original Sticht plate. These devices work much more efficiently in that they are much less prone to jamming accidentally during use.

We will consider, briefly, some of them here.

The Black Diamond ATC (air traffic controller), the DMM BUG and the HB SHERIF, all work in a similar way and are used exactly as you would use the old Sticht plate. (See vol.

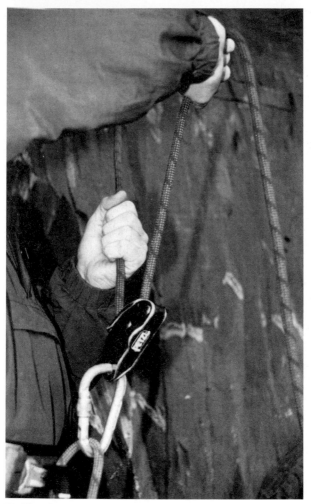
52 The Gri Gri – paying out the rope to the leader.

To leader

Grip tightly when paying out

Control / dead rope

53 The Gri Gri – the alternative method of paying out rope to a leader.

one, page 54.) There are idiosyncrasies to each. If you are using 8mm twin ropes, as you might on a big route to save on weight, the ATC does not operate efficiently if you have to hold a leader fall. You really have to grip the ropes tightly even to hold the weight of a climber. The manufacturer recommends that the device should be used on 9 mm (⅜ in) and 10.5 mm (¹³⁄₃₂ in) ropes, with which it does work extremely well.

The BUG has quite tight holes for the rope in comparison to others. This makes it a very efficient holding device but it can be a problem getting an 11 mm (⁷⁄₁₆ in) static abseil rope through the holes. This is a consideration if you use static ropes to gain access by abseil to climbs on sea cliffs for example, or on Big Wall routes. Once the rope is through the device it does operate perfectly smoothly.

Another interesting device that works along the same principles is the Wild Country Variable Controller. The wedge profile permits two levels of friction braking. If you thread the rope through so that the controlling rope is on the thin end of the wedge you achieve maximum braking effect. This should always be used for belaying a climber, the leader particularly. By having the controlling rope out of the thick side of the wedge the braking power is reduced by a fraction. This is useful for abseiling on double ropes, in particular where friction generated through the device may hinder smooth descent. In all other respects the VC is used exactly as you would any other device of this kind.

Photos 54 and 55 show each of the devices. Photos 56, 57, 58 and 59 show a sequence of taking in the rope when belaying a second. The methods of locking off a belay device illustrated in vol. one are still applicable and photos 60, 61 and 62 show another method that has become popular in recent years. With this method you do have to be very careful not to let any rope slip through the device as you are tying it off and again when releasing it whilst under load.

Wild Country
VC

Wild Country
SRC

DMM Bug

54 Belay devices.

Another device for belaying is also illustrated in photo 54. This is called the Single Rope Controller (SRC) and is also manufactured by Wild Country. The instructions that accompany the device suggest that a good deal of practice is required before you can be sure that the device can be operated efficiently – and there is a specific warning to experienced climbers who think they know everything! The warning is justified. It does take a bit of time to get used to but, having spent that time, the device is a tool worth using. Paying out the rope quickly to a leader who needs rope desperately is quite awkward to begin with. Taking in is very easy, as is lowering.

The way it works is quite clever. The rope will run freely in and out of the device when you need to take in or pay out but as soon as a load is put on the rope, a cantilever motion, instigated by the tensioning of the rope, forces the karabiner into the slot and jams the rope between a fixed bar and the krab. It is important to remember that the rope does not jam solid and if you let go of the controlling rope whilst under load, it will run through the device. This is an important aspect of use, that must be clearly understood. The device is suitable for use on climbing walls, top and bottom roping for groups, sport climbing and also for traditional climbing when using single ropes.

With all of the belay devices mentioned, and others that aren't, you'll need plenty of time to get used to operating them safely and correctly. If you don't mind clocking up a few hours of flying time on well protected climbs you'll give the second plenty of belaying practice.

Black Diamond
ATC

Petzl gri gri

55 Belay devices.

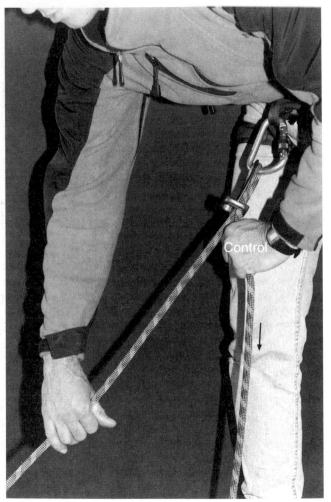

56  Taking in: Stage 1. Reach down with the live hand, pull up and pull through with the control hand at the same time.

57 Taking in: Stage 2. Lock off the controlling rope.

58 Take live hand off the live rope and hold control rope with both hands.

59 Move control hand to below live hand and go back to Stage 1.

60 Tying off a belay device: Stage 1.

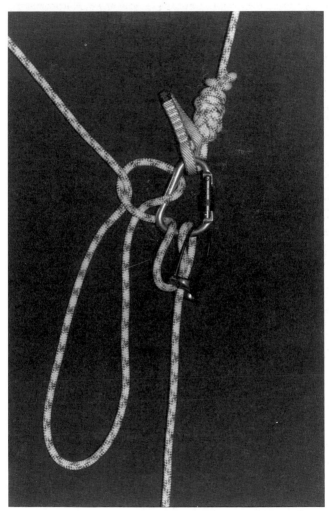

61 Tying off a belay device: Stage 2.

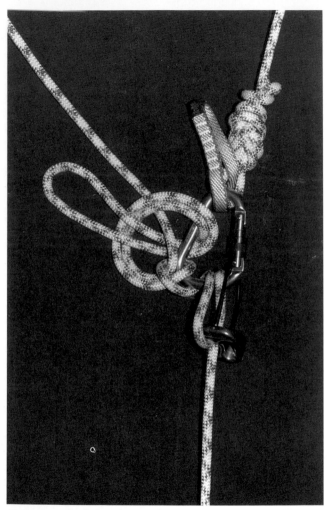

62 Tying off a belay device: Stage 3.

# HANGING STANCES

Lower grade climbs are usually blessed with large holds and commodious ledges for stances, big chunky runners aplenty and reassuringly solid anchors. As you progress to higher grades things become much less friendly and very much smaller. There is little solace to be found for a troubled mind and weary body on a tiny cramped stance at the end of a long poorly protected pitch. Neither will you find much relief on a hanging stance high above the ground, secured to your airy perch by numerous small wires, each relying on the other to take their share of the precious load they bear. Nor will you derive much pleasure from the whole experience when your ropes become snarled up in a crack far below you, or they drop into the sea or mysteriously form an unfathomable knot that no text book would ever condone.

But I make it sound far too unattractive! The gnarly experiences are mercifully few but, as any honest climber will testify, they do happen from time to time. Tiny stances and hanging belays need not turn into a nightmare of tangled ropes and awkward change-overs, provided that you arrange them methodically and work neatly.

On any small stance you will generally find it more comfortable to take some of your body weight directly on to the anchor; on a hanging stance you are, of course, forced to place yourself entirely on the anchor. Even the tiniest of ledges on which you can get a foothold will help to relieve some of the discomfort of hanging around for a long time. Modern sport climbing harnesses are not designed for such prolonged periods of hanging about and leg loops and waist belt will cut into places that you never knew could be so sensitive. Make sure that you keep adjusting your position so that cramp doesn't set in for, if it does, on the first few moves of the following pitch you will be moving as fluidly as a wooden marionette.

Where and how to store the ropes on a small cramped stance presents the biggest problem. As a general rule for most situations try not to let it drop down the crag. If you are on the edge of an overhang and the cliff is undercut below you, so that the ropes will simply hang in space, there is little chance that they will get snagged on anything. They may get a bit tangled particularly if there is a strong wind blowing, but at least you are unlikely to get them jammed. The only other time that it's safe to let them drop down the crag is if the rock below you is smooth and clear of flakes or spikes that might lure the rope causing the most hideous kind of jam. In the worst case you may be forced to descend to clear the stuck rope. If your leader is part way up a pitch, maybe on the crux of the climb and you shout up to tell them of the predicament, they will certainly not be very impressed.

Better to avoid the scenario altogether. There are a number of ways to store the rope on small stances or hanging belays. The simplest to use is to lap the rope over your feet – if you can keep them in contact with the rock (photo 63). In most cases this works very well. Keep the laps fairly short, say a maximum of 3–5 m (10–15 ft) on either side. If you make them too short there will be so many laps that they could become entangled with themselves, worse than that though they don't support themselves and will keep sliding off. Once one goes the rest usually follow with ever increasing rapidity until you find yourself in the situation you had hoped to avoid! The only inconvenience with this method will be discovered as soon as you want to adjust your foot position to a more comfortable one. Some fancy foot juggling will be needed to prevent the rope from slipping off entirely.

Another way to keep the rope secure is to lap the slack rope over the attachment to the anchor, so that it sits up against your body. Once again, make the laps about 3 m (10 ft) long, or longer if the way is clear below you. As with the previous system, there is an inconvenience. In this case it makes hand-

63 Hanging stance with the rope lapped around the feet.

ling of the belay device fairly awkward and will need considerable practice to perfect. Photos 64 and 65 show a way to do this. Notice that the rope is stored in between the belay device and the rock – it is much easier to let it run off without snagging.

You can lap the spare rope over spikes or flakes that are close to the stance in a similar way or you can lap it in your hands and then clip it to the anchor with a long sling. Clip one end of the sling into a separate krab on the anchor, pass the sling under the laps and then clip the other end into the krab. This has the great advantage of keeping the rope well out of the way. This method is particularly useful at the start of a climb on a sea cliff where there may not be a ledge onto which you can uncoil the rope.

Whichever system you use to lap the ropes, it is worth making each lap slightly shorter than the previous. This will ensure that the loops of rope do not get snagged on each other and everything will run much more smoothly (photo 66). With all the slack rope piled around you in one of the above methods, change-overs at stances may be troublesome. If you are sharing leads with your partner the rope need not be changed around because their end of the rope *should* run smoothly off the lapping. It probably won't, but that's life! If, on the other hand, you are not swapping leads you will definitely need to run the rope through so that your end is back on the top of the pile. It's good advice not to simply lift off the laps and hand them to your second. Much better to feed it lap by lap to your belayer who can then arrange it neatly.

In order to effect this as efficiently as possible try to ensure that the stance is well organised and prepared for the arrival of the second. This means having something for them to clip into directly on gaining the stance. If you have a number of different anchor points try bringing them altogether to form one central point of attachment. See methods of bringing anchors to one point in Chapter 2, pages 238 and 239, photos 2 and 3, and vol. one, page 122, photo 55.

64 Rope lapped over tie in to anchor on hanging stance.

65 Rope lapping between belay device and ropes to the anchor.

One of the most worrying aspects of a hanging stance, or any cramped stance, is the thought that your second might fall off and the load will come directly on to you. Inevitably, on such stances you are more than likely to be facing into the crag. It is more comfortable to hold a second if you are facing out from the crag but this is rarely achievable when most of your weight is directly on to the anchors. You might be able to run the rope to your second down between your legs. In doing so, if the second falls off, the loading is likely to come directly on to the anchor. But there are many circumstances where this is simply neither convenient nor possible.

A useful trick is to run the live rope through a runner above you. Obviously this must be a hundred per cent solid runner, as it will need to bear pretty much the full force of a falling second (photo 67). If your anchor is absolutely bombproof, and only if, you can run the rope through a separate karabiner attached directly to the whole anchor. In both cases any loading on you as the belayer will come from an upwards direction and the extra friction created by the rope running through the krab will greatly reduce the load you have to hold. It is important to remember here that the krab through which the second's rope will run sits perfectly perpendicular to the rock. If it naturally lies flat against the rock, pulling the rope through it will create a twisting action that will result in a kinked and tangled climbing rope. It basically twists the inner core of the rope inside the sheath and can ruin an otherwise perfectly good rope.

On leaving a hanging stance it is very important that the leader places a running belay as soon as possible. If no decent runner is available, consider using one of the anchors as the first runner. A leader who falls directly on to the belayer can easily generate a fall factor of 2 (see page 305).

It is important to take time out to practise these suggestions before you get yourself into a really scary position. This can be done on any smallish stance on easier climbs, even though you

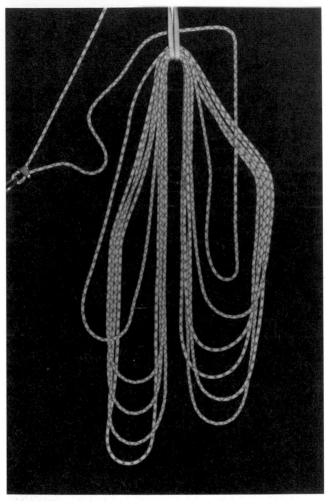

66 The principle of rope lapping using ever decreasing lengths of lap.

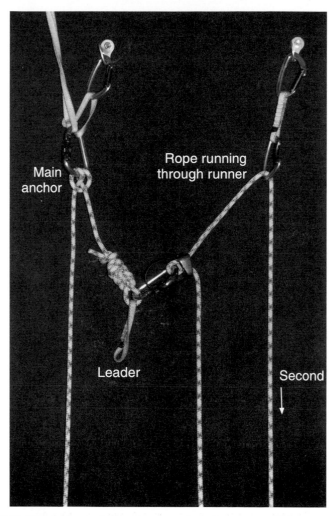

67 Taking in through a runner on a hanging stance. Make sure it's a good one!

might be able to stand comfortably and have enough room to coil the rope on the ledge. Just remember to be neat and methodical!

## DOUBLE ROPE TECHNIQUE

In the first volume of *Modern Rope Techniques* I briefly discussed some of the principles of double rope technique. British climbers are probably amongst the few nationalities in the climbing world that use double ropes for the vast majority of their climbing whether on rock or snow and ice.

There are distinct advantages in using two ropes to safeguard a climb. The most vaunted advantage is that it is better in terms of arranging protection. A climb that zig-zags its way up the rock face will be a problem to protect if using a single rope because, inevitably, you will need runners in places that create angles in the way that the rope runs. Not only will this increase the friction and make the rope difficult to drag up the pitch, it will also heighten the possibility that some runners may be pulled out if the leader, or second for that matter, takes a fall.

Using double ropes allows the leader to place protection off to one side of the climb and, by careful management, arrange the ropes to run in relatively straight lines. It also makes it easier to protect traverses for both leader and second with adequate runner placements and reduced rope drag.

There are other advantages. Psychologically it makes things feel a lot safer. You know when you are pulling up the rope to make a critical clip into a runner, that you are not increasing the likelihood of a longer fall if you are unfortunate enough to fall off whilst attempting the clip.

It also makes retreating from a climb or abseiling off considerably more efficient in that you are able to abseil the full length of the rope if need be. Using single ropes only permits an abseil of half the full rope's length.

Tying into anchors is also more straightforward. If you have two anchors, one rope can be tied into each, and even third and fourth anchors are simpler to attach to. This offers added security to the climb.

Belaying is only a little more complex (see page 348) and with a little practice can quickly be mastered.

You do need to be a little more attentive to the way in which the ropes are organised to avoid complicated and annoying twists developing. It is very easy to set off on a climb with the ropes running perfectly but by pitch three have them in such a tangle that the only solution is to untie from one and pull it through the twists. Lots of twists will also have an effect on running belays. If the twists run a couple of metres up the rope in front of you when you are seconding there is a chance that they might pull out runners as the leader takes in. If these runners are critical, on a traverse for example, it may induce a greater feeling of insecurity than might be desired.

Twists are introduced into the system every time you turn a complete circle. Tie in to two ropes and see what happens when you spin around three or four times. Imagine doing this whilst on a climb or particularly on a stance and you will soon realise how those twists develop so 'mysteriously'. Being aware of the problem goes a long way to preventing it happening in the first instance.

Try to make sure that you run the ropes through at the end of each pitch. Do them individually if you can be bothered or at least together and separate them by running one finger in between each rope as you do so. If twists are apparent one of you can spin around to unravel them. Don't do it too fast or you'll get dizzy and fall off the ledge!

Take a good look at the pitch before you set off and plan where you hope to place runners and which rope you will use where. A moment's planning pays dividends in the long run.

Double ropes provide considerably safer opportunities to protect both leader and second on traverses. Using a single rope may require you to miss out using a crucial runner because to place it would create too much friction or pull out other more critical runners. Such problems can be avoided by extending runners with long slings to decrease the angles through which the rope runs, but doing so sometimes means that a fall may be longer than you would like. Double ropes permit better use of runners in such situations and, though sometimes runners may need to be extended, the occasions are far fewer.

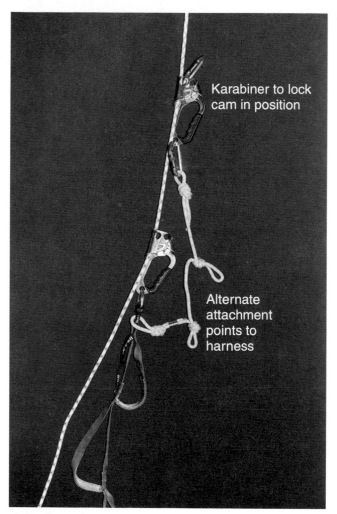

Karabiner to lock cam in position

Alternate attachment points to harness

68 Traditional method of ascending a fixed rope. Note that the foot ascendeur is connected back to the harness.

# 9 Ascending a Fixed Rope

In vol. one the techniques of ascending a fixed rope were discussed briefly. Though all that was said remains valid, there are one or two further suggestions worth making.

Whenever you have a need to ascend a fixed rope other than in an improvised rescue scenario, you should consider using some kind of a mechanical ascending device. Such devices not only offer increased security but they are also much more efficient to use.

Occasions that demand the use of mechanical devices include those in which an instructor is teaching a student to lead and those where you are on a multi-day climb that requires you to descend and re-ascend on several occasions. Both these require a slightly different approach to the method in which you attach yourself to the devices.

For ascending a fixed rope when climbing on big walls, it is advisable to connect yourself via the sit harness to both devices as a sensible safety measure. Photo 68 shows a suggested method of doing this. You would be well advised to use a chest harness connected to the sit harness and to link the two together to form on central point of attachment. This will make long ascents considerably more comfortable and provides a better positioned point of attachment if you have a heavy load on your back.

The length of the safety back up attachment to the foot ascendeur is fairly critical and should be adjusted so as not to impede the distance that you can move the foot ascendeur up the rope for maximum efficiency.

There are a large number of devices available for ascending a fixed rope. Those that incorporate a handle are the most comfortable to use over a long period of time. Lighter versions are also available that do not feature a handle and are worth considering for short sections of ascent. Petzl is perhaps the most well known brand name and offers a range of devices which will suit any situation you are likely to encounter.

The Croll is an interesting device that is designed to connect between a sit harness and a chest harness. Photo 69 shows how the Croll should be used. It is a very efficient device in that there is no need to move it up the rope by hand. As you stand up in the foot loop the device slides along the rope. It is important to fix the Croll securely at both ends, the top to a chest harness and the bottom to the sit harness. Ensure that there is very little slack in the connection. This will help it to operate as efficiently as it is designed to do. Another important development is the Ropeman from Wild Country. This remarakable little device is incredibly simple to use and offers a degree of safety and efficiency unsurpassed for its diminutive appearance. It weighs only a few grammes and can be carried easily in place of a prusik loop, over which it has considerable advantage, particularly in aspects of safety. Photo 70 shows the Ropeman attached to the rope. As a device to use in emergency prusiking, such as crevasse or crag rescues, it is particularly useful.

If the rock is low-angled where you can support a good deal of your body weight on your feet, you need only attach yourself to the Ropeman via the abseil loop on your harness. Make the attachment fairly short. As you step up the rock face, take hold of the fixed rope below the device and pull it upwards. The rope will run smoothly through the Ropeman and you can feel secure, knowing that you are able to lean back on it at any time and it will lock on the rope.

If you have two devices and the ground is much steeper, attach to the top Ropeman via your harness and use the bottom one for a foot loop. Don't make the connection to the sit harness too long, about level with your chest is plenty. The foot loop attachment should be as short as you can comfortably stand up in. Move the top Ropeman up by sliding your hand under the cam and pushing it back so that it releases.

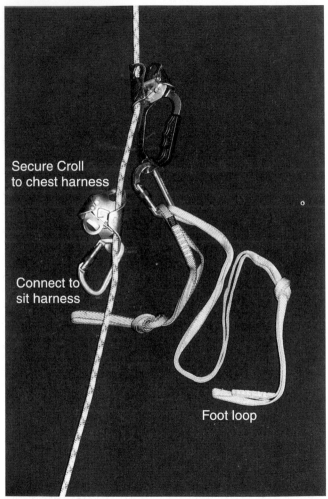

Secure Croll
to chest harness

Connect to
sit harness

Foot loop

69 Ascending a rope using a Croll. The Croll must be firmly
attached to a chest harness of some sort.

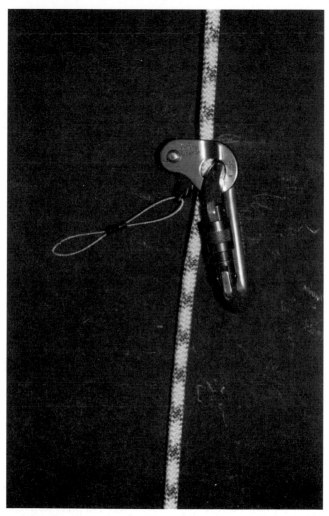

70 The Wild Country Ropeman – a superb little device.

To move the foot one up, keep a little tension on the device and take hold of the rope below the device. By pulling upwards on the rope the Ropeman will slide up perfectly.

There is no reason why the Ropeman could not be used by instructors teaching lead climbing (see page 300), instead of a more traditional type of ascendeur. The grip on the rope is just as efficient and the strength of the device as adequate. If you are not happy to do this, it can be used as a back up to another ascending device by placing it above the main ascendeur and connecting the two together with a karabiner.

71  Ascending a fixed rope. When carrying a big pack always
wear a chest harness.

# 10  Retreating from Climbs

Just as there will be success on climbs, there will also be failures. Learning to cope with failing on a climb is a difficult thing, particularly if the route is one you've aspired to, dreamt about doing and sought as much information on as you can.

Talking about failure seems a very negative thing but when you're out on your own having to make decisions about backing off a route, it takes on monumental importance.

One of my early failures on a climb was on a route at the Roaches when I was at college in Buxton. I was the only climber on our course and keen to encourage others to climb so that I would always have partners to go out with. I can't remember for the life of me the name of the climb but it was away left of the Sloth area. It was a bleak and miserable autumn day with a fine drizzle dampening everything but our enthusiasm. Not having a guidebook, we scoured the crag for likely looking easy lines and found one that looked possible. It began reasonably enough but the rock was slimy and cold. About 10 m (30–35 ft) or so off the ground, maybe less, further progress became a matter for bravery that I was unable to muster and I decided to retreat.

I had put a sling around an almost horizontal spike of rock for protection and worked out that, if I took that off, I could put the rope around it and be lowered off by the guys holding the rope below. They didn't know how to use a waist belay so all three of them just held on to the rope. All went well until about 3 m (10 ft) off the ground when one of them noticed the rope gradually creeping off the spike. We stopped and pondered our next move and decided that it would probably be OK until I reached the ground. Of course, it wasn't – just as soon as they resumed lowering me it popped right off. I fell down on top of my companions and all four of us tumbled and rolled down the muddy slope in a tangled heap with much mirth and merriment. Only one of them ever went climbing again after that. Another instructional success!

Retreating off a pitch when you're part way up and have reached the point where you can get no further can be quite harrowing. If you have a good runner you may well decide to lower off that and then let your partner make an attempt. If he or she doesn't fancy having a go at leading the pitch you'll either have to down climb taking out all the runners as you descend or, if the prospect of down climbing is too daunting, you'll need to lower off a piece of gear, or even two connected together.

This may present you with a bit of a dilemma on two counts. One is of pride. Anything you leave behind is a reminder of your failure and a symbol of a failure for others to gloat upon. The other is the loss of an expensive piece of equipment that might have been hard to come by. Put both out of your mind, for the thing that matters most of all is that you get off safely and return to climb another day.

When being lowered off you should always be lowered with the rope running through a karabiner. Never be tempted to run the rope through a nylon sling or through the wire of a nut. Nylon has a very low melting point and with the added weight and the friction of the rope running over a nylon sling it is possible to generate sufficient heat to melt through the sling. Lowering through a wire doesn't create the same problems but the rope will not run smoothly over such a tiny radius and you may well damage the climbing rope – a much more expensive item of gear to replace.

It is far better to leave behind a krab. It need not be one of your best though – in fact make sure it isn't. It's quite a good idea to carry your nut key on an old krab which you could use for just such a purpose. Although you might lose a nut or a sling at least you'll feel that that's all you've lost.

If you are part way up a multi-pitch climb, say on the third pitch, once you've been lowered back to the stance you'll then need to find an escape route that is considerably easier or, if none exist, retreat to the ground by abseil.

It is quite likely you'll need to leave gear behind on each abseil. If you can get back to the ground in one long abseil, then all is well and good and you'll lose only minimal gear. If, on the other hand, you're too high off the ground to do this, you'll need to go down in stages. Unless you have a clear view of where to go and can see likely places to use as staging posts, it may be safer to retreat down the line of ascent. This becomes less preferable if the route you climbed weaves its way all over the crag.

When you retreat by abseil in this way there is no need to leave a krab behind on each anchor. The rope will be doubled through the anchor and will only run over the nylon sling when you retrieve it. At this point you no longer need the sling and so any heat generated that might melt the sling is of little consequence. Of course, you may not have to leave anything behind if there are suitable rock spikes to abseil off, or maybe trees. If you use spikes in this way make sure that the first person down tests the rope to see that it will pull around the spike before the last person sets off. If it doesn't, you may well have to leave a bit of gear in place to make the retrieval of the rope less troublesome.

On long multi-pitch descents off big routes, and particularly the most popular ones, you may find that all the equipment is in place. There is a climb on the Grauewand for example, just above the Furka Pass in Switzerland, where the abseil descent has been rigged with two large ring bolts connected with a plate that has an eye in the end for clipping in to. This is the most luxurious of pre-set rap stations. Many others may feature in-situ gear connected with a chain or with slings. Regardless of the set-up each should be checked before you use them, rather than blindly trusting to them.

In the case of all metal anchors there is very little that can go wrong, unless of course they are old and rusted through.

Slings, however are a very different matter. Nylon deteriorates over a period of time when exposed to the UV rays of the sun. Any piece of in-situ gear that is faded ought to be treated with suspicion. To check the degree of fading unravel a bit of the knot and see what the original colour of the sling was. Similarly, if the rope is to be threaded through the sling directly, some heat will be generated when ropes are pulled through during retrieval. This heat may cause some melting of the nylon and this could weaken the sling considerably.

If you need to replace the sling do so with careful consideration not just to how you will use it but also how others might use it in the future. Normally at least two anchors will be used. When connecting the two make sure that you arrange the sling so that, if one were to fail, your abseil rope will not detach itself from the other. Photo 48 shows a suggested set-up. There are other ways to connect the two to one point and the principles remain the same for whatever method you choose.

I once, to the horror of my partner, suggested that we abseil off a lace from my rock boot. It was 4mm nylon boot lace and we did thread it through the peg about eight times before joining the ends together. Nonetheless, when I think back on it now it was a pretty stupid thing to have done, even abseiling off one old peg was daft enough. It came down to the fact that I didn't want to leave anything of value behind.

From then on, to cope with such eventualities in the future, I began carrying a couple of short prusik loops made up of 6mm accessory cord – and have been doing ever since. Boot laces aren't what they used to be anyway . . .

Retreating off bolted climbs when you fail can be a bit troublesome. Bolt hangers that allow you to clip in two karabiners at the same time, or even to thread a rope through, are much more convenient to retreat from without leaving gear behind. Take the most simplistic scenario: a bolt climb with large ring bolts or DMM Eco anchors. With these it is a simple enough matter to clip yourself to the bolt with a short cow's tail attachment made up from a quick draw. Secure the climbing rope to your harness and then untie from the end of the rope. Thread the end through the bolt and tie back on. Ask your partner belaying you to take all your weight on the climbing rope and then unclip the cow's tail from the bolt. Some jiggling of krab and rope may be needed but this is easily accomplished. You can then be lowered through the bolt and collect the other quick draws on the way down.

If you are climbing a sport route that has any other type of hanger you have bigger problems and will need to leave something behind to lower off, though if the crag is easily accessed from above, you can simply nip around to the top and abseil down to retrieve the lost runner. Or you might be able to ask the next person to climb the route if they would kindly get it back for you.

If neither of the above solutions is possible you should leave a krab behind on the bolt and be lowered off that. You may be loathe to leave a good krab behind, in which case you must take one that you are prepared to leave, unclip the quick draw and then clip the disposable krab into the bolt hanger, with the climbing rope already clipped in. To do this you'll need to have enough strength to hold yourself on the rock whilst re-arranging the gear.

Another way to retreat is to clip yourself into the bolt with a cow's tail. Take a short length of cord/prusik loop and thread it through the hanger. Take the climbing rope and tie the two ends of the cord together, thus securing the rope. It is probably advisable to thread the cord through twice so that you have double the strength.

Next, pull the rope through, so that you have enough to reach the ground or the stance below on the doubled rope. Having done that you can attach yourself to both ropes in preparation to abseil off. You will, of course, need a device to descend on, normally your belay device. Once the abseil is rigged you can untie from the end of the rope and let it drop to the ground. Unclip from the bolt and cow's tail attachment, clear any other gear and descend. Photos 72, 73 and 74 show the procedure.

This same principle can be applied to a retreat off any kind of runner, provided, of course, that you are happy with the placement!

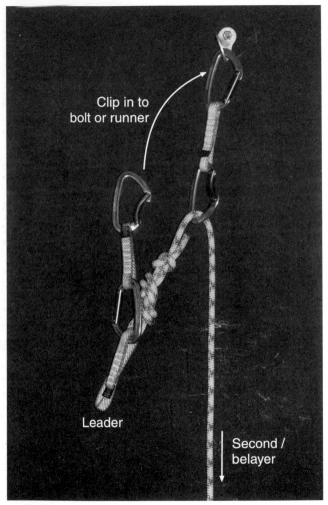

**Clip in to
bolt or runner**

**Leader**

**Second /
belayer**

72  Retreating from a single bolt or runner whilst still hanging on it: Stage 1.

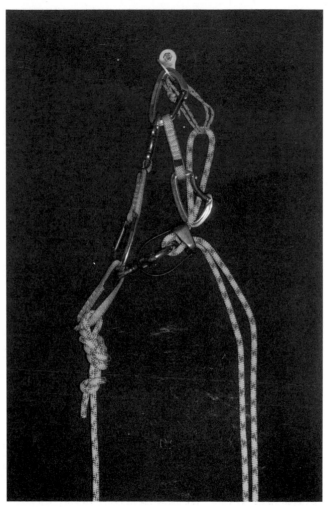

73  Retreating from a single bolt or runner whilst still hanging on it: Stage 2.

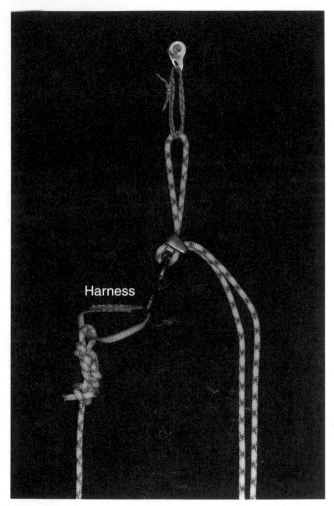

74 Retreating from a single bolt or runner whilst still hanging on it: Stage 3.

# 11 Miscellany

## TENSIONING ROPES FOR A TYROLEAN OR SAFETY LINE

In the first volume, *Modern Rope Techniques*, I suggested that ropes could be tensioned using pulleys at each turning point in the tensioning system. Whilst this makes it considerably easier to attain the required tension, the pulleys used have a limitation to their breaking strength. This limitation is imposed by the strength of the axle on which the pulley rotates.

If you do not have pulleys or those that you have do not fall within acceptable safety margins, the technique illustrated in photos 75, 76 and 77 is a perfectly good method of tensioning ropes.

The Alpine butterfly knot is tied as far down the rope as you can possibly reach. Try to make the loop formed by the knot fairly small, just large enough to squeeze your fist through.

Attach a screwgate karabiner. Take the rope from the knot and pass it through a screwgate on the anchor, then take it back to the Alpine butterfly krab and clip it in. You now have a pulling system. It might require a number of people to pull on the rope to achieve the required tension.

Once the rope is as tight as you need it to be, 'marry' the ropes and then secure them by threading a bight of rope through the krab at the anchor and tie a number of half hitches around the three tensioned ropes. You can include the fourth if you wish but there is really no need.

As stated in vol. one, it is important to try to use low-stretch ropes for this type of work as they are considerably more robust and capable of the loads exerted on them.

Over a period of use, some tension may be lost and you'll need to re-tension the rope from time to time. This is effected

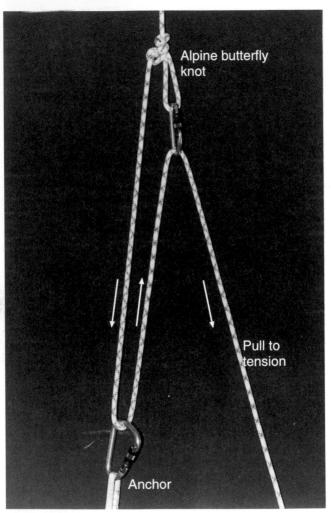

75 Tensioning ropes: Stage 1.

76 Tensioning ropes: Stage 2.

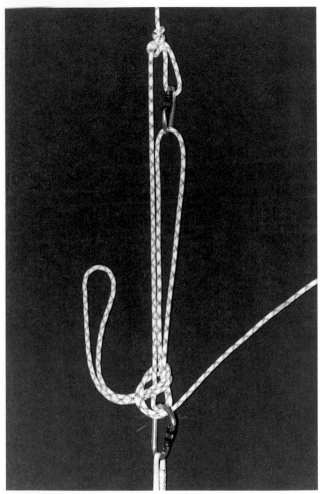

77 Tensioning ropes: Stage 3: 'Marry' the ropes and secure with half hitches.

easily by releasing the half hitches whilst 'marrying' the ropes together and then getting help to pull more tension into the system. The Alpine butterfly will be extremely tight after use and may be difficult to undo. If the ropeway has been used to cross a river or a gorge and you need to get the rope across to one side without getting it wet or without the risk of getting it stuck around a rock or a tree, for example, the best way to do it is as follows.

Decide which side the rope needs to end up on. On that side take in all the rope until the person left on the other side has only the end of rope to hold. Both sides then pull the rope until there is tension in it, but only holding it in their hands. On a pre-arranged signal the person on the opposite side lets go of the rope and, in theory, it should go whistling over to the side you want it to finish up on. Obviously, those receiving the rope must be prepared for the sudden slackness otherwise they will fall flat on their backsides – usually accompanied by much mirth and merriment from onlookers.

## SAFETY LINES FOR TRAVERSES

In any situation, such as a sea level traverse for example, where you need to rig a horizontal safety line, those for whom the line is rigged will need to have some method of clipping in. There are various ways of doing this and the simplest is to clip in with a sling attached to the harness.

It is vitally important that you consider carefully how the line is rigged. For safety it is preferable not to have too much slack in the system, otherwise the purpose of the line is defeated. Clearly, the line is there to hold someone if they clip off. To do this the line needs to have a reasonable amount of tension in it, otherwise the fall could be considerably longer than is desired and might lead to injury.

It is no good, therefore, to stretch a rope between two points that are a long way apart, 20 m (65 ft) for example. In fact, I

would venture to suggest that the maximum distance acceptable ought to be around the 6 m (20 ft) mark, particularly if you
are using climbing ropes to rig the safety line. Anyone loading
on a horizontally placed line will inevitably introduce considerable stretch and this must be considered when rigging. Low
stretch ropes present less of a problem in this respect but
nonetheless the same considerations must be applied. You
must therefore, make sure that the rope is anchored securely
and at frequent intervals.

Anchors placed along the traverse would, ideally, be above
the line of travel. This is not always possible. Any anchors
placed on the line of travel should be placed so that they
cannot be lifted out accidentally. To this end you might need
to rig an upward pulling anchor to hold the downward pulling
one under tension, so that it remains solidly placed.

The knot that you use to attach the rope to each of these
anchors could either be an overhand, a figure eight or an
Alpine butterfly. It matters little, though the overhand, and
particularly the Alpine butterfly, are more suited to taking a
load in either direction.

The change-over at each anchor point is effected with greater
safety if you arrange a cow's tail similar to that shown in photo
78. By using this set-up you will be secure on one rope whilst
you clip into the next. As you arrive at an anchor the spare
cow's tail is clipped in and the screwgate secured before you
unclip from the other.

Not all safety lines rigged this way are horizontal. Inevitably
there will be sections of vertical ascent or descent. The Via
Ferrata of the Italian Alps are classic examples of this.

If you take a fall in ascent or descent you will obviously fall
as far as the anchor point below you. In some cases this might
be a considerable distance. The forces generated by such a fall
are enormous. For example, if the length of sling attachment is
1 m (3 ft) long and you fall 5 m (15 ft) the fall factor (see page 305)
is 5. It is made doubly worse by the fact that there is no shock

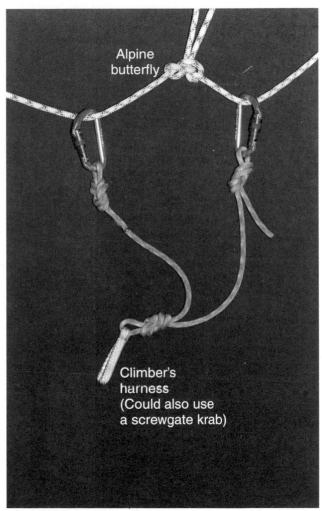

Alpine
butterfly

Climber's
harness
(Could also use
a screwgate krab)

78 A simple cow's tail attachment for safety line traverses.

absorption in the system. If the sling that attaches you to the line doesn't break, your body is almost certain to.

There are a number of devices that are specifically designed to absorb the shock of such a fall. The least complex of all is the ZYPER from Petzl. This is a very simple set up constructed of a length of rope with pre-formed loops in either end. Shock absorption is effected by a simple twist through the link that is attached to the harness. Basically, as the load comes on to the lanyard, the rope slips gradually through the link, absorbing a great deal of the shock load.

Such devices cannot be improvised easily from normal climbing equipment.

## RETRIEVABLE SINGLE ROPE ABSEIL

Quite when this technique may be useful is difficult to say with any certainty. It's one of those things that may come in useful sometime – like that bizarre tool stashed away in the shed that'll come in handy if I never use it!

However, I did hear an interesting story from a mate of mine who was climbing in Spain once. Arriving at the top of a multi-pitch climb, he waited to one side while the pair in front rigged their abseil descent. The first climber went down and the second climber attached himself to the rope to begin the descent. As he leant backwards on to the rope my mate noticed that he was only attached to one rope and frantically lunged forward to save him, screaming, 'Stop, stop, you're only on one rope!' The climber turned to him, slightly bemused by the show of concern, and said, 'I know. My belay device will only take one rope.' He'd rigged the rope out of sight of my mate who wasn't able to see the whole set up. Photo 79 shows the method clearly.

There are two vitally important considerations. The first is that the ring or maillon or krab that the rope is threaded through must not have too large a hole, otherwise the knot

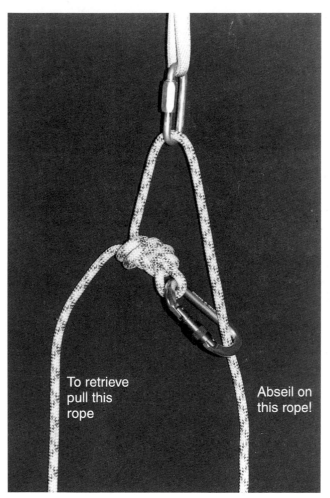

To retrieve
pull this
rope

Abseil on
this rope!

79  Retrievable single rope abseil. Make sure that you abseil on
the correct rope!

might slip through as you descend. Whilst it will never become entirely detached, it may become jammed in the hole or cause confusion over which rope to pull.

Most important of all, though, is to ensure that you abseil on the correct rope – the opposite side to that in which the knot is tied. The consequences of going down on the wrong rope do not bear thinking about.

# Glossary of terms used in the text

*Anchor*

Point of security on a cliff. Can be anything from natural chockstones to Friends. To secure oneself to the crag or mountain.

*Assisted Evacuation*

Rescuer evacuates a victim who is incapacitated and unable to help in any useful way.

*Assisted Hoist*

Victim helps the rescuer to pull him/herself up the cliff.

*Autobloc*

A device that will lock around a rope and prevent slippage when a load is applied to the rope in a particular direction. It must also be capable of releasing itself when the rope is pulled the opposite way.

*Belaying*

The way in which a climber's rope is safeguarded whilst he or she is climbing. For example a belay plate or an Italian hitch.

*Central Loop*

The loop that is formed by the climbing rope when it is tied into a harness.

*Dead Rope or Slack Rope*

Any rope that does not have a climber directly on the end of it.

*Doubled Snaplinks*

Two snaplinks clipped in with the gates on opposite sides used for safety instead of a screwgate karabiner.

*Escape from the System*

The technique of releasing oneself from the belay system and end of rope whilst ensuring the safety of the climber you are responsible for.

*Hanging Hoist*

The technique of relieving the the weight from the end of the rope whilst someone is hanging on it.

*In Situ*

Abbreviation for in situation i.e. gear that is already in place.

*Jumaring*

Ascending a fixed rope using mechanical devices.

*Load or Live Rope*

Any rope that has a climber directly on the end of it.

*Multiple Anchors*

More than one anchor point.

*Passing a Knot*

The technique of passing the join of two ropes through an abseiling or lowering device.

*'Prusik'*

Any knot that will grip on to a thicker rope when a load is applied.

*Prusiking*

Ascending a fixed rope with any kind of 'prusik' knot.

*Safety Back-Up*

A back-up system should the main system fail.

*Stance*

A ledge or place where one anchors oneself to belay a climbing companion.

*Tail end*

The rope left over after tying a knot in the end of a rope.

*Tie on loops*

The loops of a harness through which the manufacturer recommends the rope to be threaded to tie into the harness.

*Tying Off*

The technique of securing a rope that is part of a belaying, abseiling or lowering system. It is also the method used to attach to pitons, both ice and rock, that haven't been inserted right up to the hilt.

*Tying On*

Fixing a climbing rope to a harness. Also used with reference to securing a climber to an anchor or anchor points.

*Unassisted Hoist*

The situation in which the rescuer hoists a victim who is incapacitated and unable to help in any useful way.

# Index

Figures in *italic* indicate illustrations.